☞ The Enduring Seminoles

The Florida History and Culture Series

Florida A&M University, Tallahassee
Florida Atlantic University, Boca Raton
Florida Gulf Coast University, Ft. Myers
Florida International University, Miami
Florida State University, Tallahassee
New College of Florida, Sarasota
University of Central Florida, Orlando
University of Florida, Gainesville
University of North Florida, Jacksonville
University of South Florida, Tampa
University of West Florida, Pensacola

THE ENDURING SEMINOLES

From Alligator Wrestling to Casino Gambling,
Revised and Expanded Edition

Patsy West

Foreword by Gary R. Mormino and Raymond Arsenault

University Press of Florida
Gainesville/Tallahassee/Tampa/Boca Raton
Pensacola/Orlando/Miami/Jacksonville/Ft. Myers/Sarasota

LIBRARY OF CONGRESS CATALOGING-IN-PUBLICATION DATA
West, Patsy, 1947–
The enduring Seminoles: from alligator wrestling to ecotourism / Patsy West.
p. cm. —(The Florida history and culture series)
Includes bibliographical references (p.) and index.
ISBN 978-0-8130-3213-9 (pbk)
1. Mikasuki Indians—Economic conditions. 2. Seminole Indians—Economic
conditions. 3. Mikasuki Indians—Ethnic identity. 4. Seminole Indians—Ethnic
identity. 5. Tourist trade—Florida. I. Title. II. Series.
E99.M615W47   1998
330.9759'0089973—dc21   98-26996

The University Press of Florida is the scholarly publishing agency for the State
University System of Florida, comprising Florida A&M University, Florida
Atlantic University, Florida Gulf Coast University, Florida International
University, Florida State University, New College of Florida, University of
Central Florida, University of Florida, University of North Florida, University
of South Florida, and University of West Florida.

University Press of Florida
15 Northwest 15th Street
Gainesville, FL 32611-2079
http://www.upf.com

This book is dedicated to the Seminoles on Exhibition and to those who aided them in their early endeavors.

CONTENTS

PHOTOGRAPHS AND MAPS

MAPS

The trajectory of the Seminole and Miccosukee Tribes in twentieth-century Florida almost defies comprehension. If Florida was the least populated southern state in 1900, Seminoles and Miccosukees added few inhabitants to the census rolls. For much of the late nineteenth and early twentieth centuries, Florida newspapers and agency reports predicted the imminent demise, if not extinction, of Native American inhabitants and their culture. In 1914, as a far-away war in Europe began to be felt in South Florida, an Indian agent reported, "The Indians, some 600 in number, have been hit harder than any other people in the country." Four years later, an observer noted in the *Fort Myers Press*, "The days of the Seminole canoe are numbered and with it comes a change in his mode of living." Eight decades later, who could have imagined that the most famous Y2K party in Florida would be held at an Indian "reservation"? On December 31, 1999, over 75,000 visitors gathered at the Big Cypress Indian Reservation to cheer the rock band Phish. What a century! What a story!

As the 2006–7 Great Drought and headlines that the Seminole Tribe had purchased the Hard Rock Café for almost one billion dollars suggest, it seems that Seminole canoes and modes of living proved to be far more enduring and resourceful than commentators ever imagined. Patsy West's revised and expanded edition of *The Enduring Seminoles: From Alligator Wrestling to Casino Gaming* is most welcome. Much has happened since the 1998 publication of her seminal book. West's new materials elaborate upon the remarkable cultural and entrepreneurial skills of modern Miccosukee leaders. West's profile of the charismatic and controversial Seminole leader Chief James Billie is engaging and enlightening. His legacy is emboldened by a new wave of gleaming gaming casinos and rising revenues. Consider that when Chief James Billie took over in 1979, the Tribe's budget was $500,000 a year. By the time he was removed from power in 2001, that figure had exploded to $650 million. Readers should not be surprised at recent reports that Seminole and Miccosukee tourist establishments are having difficulties recruiting workers—Native American, American, or immigrant—to wrestle alligators!

Gary Mormino and Raymond Arsenault
Series Editors

For much of the twentieth century, Seminole tourism seen in simple Indian village venues was the lifeblood economy that defined the cultural economic endeavors of the Native Americans today known as the Florida Seminole and Miccosukee Indians. Their involvement in the tourist market, which began early in that century, nurtured and enhanced traditional and cultural elements of their tribalism. A crafts market and the popular crowd pleaser alligator wrestling were introduced aspects of tourism. Over the decades these new economic elements became part and parcel of tribal culture. Significant relationships between the Seminoles and tourism have existed over the decades, specifically in the areas of economics, culture, art, and politics. By the 1960s, however, the tourist economy began to wane. The Tribes' entry into gaming, beginning with the Seminole Tribe's bingo operations in 1979, bolstered their near poverty level existence, becoming a highly profitable aspect of tribal tourism. Then, in December 2006, the Seminole Tribe of Florida gained a global tourist market with the purchase of Hard Rock International, which includes gaming casinos, restaurants, and retail outlets in forty-five countries and boasts the world's largest collection of music memorabilia. All of these important aspects of tribal tourism are addressed in *The Enduring Seminoles*.

Early in the twentieth century when the reticent *i:laponathli:* (*Mika-suki*-speaking Seminoles) began their involvement with tourism, their economic plight was desperate. Their trade economy had begun a seemingly unending decline. Their environment was changing before their eyes as the eastern Everglades was drained for agriculture and south Florida began to develop rapidly around them. The impact of the tourist market on the native population was so strong that even the smaller enclave of Creek Seminoles around Lake Okeechobee began to adopt the economic advantages of tourism. In the late 1940s and 1950s, the tourist craft market continued to be of major economic importance, and most families were involved in craft sales to bolster their income.

While continuing to participate in the tourist market, today the Seminole and Miccosukee tribes are entering a new phase of tourism involvement, one supported and enhanced by the income from lucrative tribal enterprises such as "high stakes bingo." Tribally owned and operated enterprises are in full swing. Even though not all tribal members are directly involved, cultural tourism—the sharing and displaying of certain highly visible aspects of their touristic experience—serves to reinforce a tribe's group identity. Tourism will continue to be a major tribal enterprise as the Seminoles and Miccosukees enter the twenty-first century.

Yet, none of this enthusiasm for a tourist-dependent economy was evident when I began this study some fifteen years ago. Even earlier, as a youth in the late 1950s, I was exposed to the popular Florida Writers' Project / Department of Agriculture Bulletin *Seminole Indians in Florida*, which contained information on the Seminoles collected from materials from the late 1930s and early 1940s. It portrayed the tourist attractions that featured Seminoles, as well as the Seminole participants themselves, in an unfavorable light. When I became a museum curator in the early 1970s, my study of the Florida Indians intensified and I read the 1931 "Survey of the Seminole Indians of Florida," Senate Document 314, by Roy Nash. This work also explicitly condemned the idea of Seminoles on exhibition. The authors of these two major sources of information set the tone for future condemnation of the tourist economy and of the individuals who benefitted from its income.

Not until 1980, when I interviewed Henry Coppinger, Jr., a pioneer in the Seminole exhibition business, his associate Phil James, and his contemporary Alan W. Davis, was I exposed to an opposing view. They were kindhearted persons, full of admiration and love for the Seminoles. In their seventies, Coppinger and Davis still kept up with some Seminole families whom I also knew.

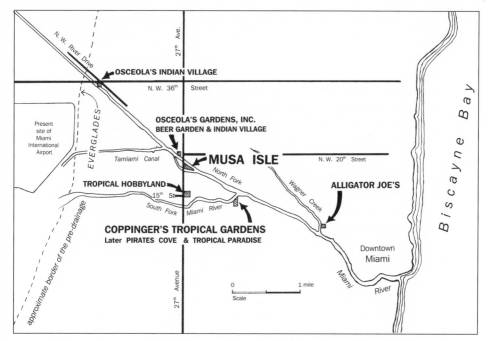

1. Downtown Miami, showing the locations of the major Seminole Indian Village tourist attractions where the *i.laponathli:* were employed. Included for contrast is the border of the predrainage Everglades and the present site of today's Miami International Airport. By David M. Blackard.

I discussed the tourist attraction experience with the older generation of Seminole men who spoke English and did not find them to be at all negative or apologetic about their former life on exhibition. They viewed it as the "good old days." Cory Osceola, one of Coppinger's employees from the early years of the business, told me in 1975, "Yeah, I tried to look Henry Coppinger up last time I was by" (Osceola 1975).

The emerging pros and cons led me to reexamine the nature of the early tourist attractions in the hope of attaining an accurate picture, good or bad. Since the government's negative views were public record, I concentrated on an opposing source of information, interviews with employees of the tourist attractions, Indian and non-Indian. A vast collection of newspaper accounts made it possible to reconstruct this important but unexplored economic and cultural era early in the twentieth century and discuss the impact of tourism on tribal lives prior to the tribal gaming and leisure activities that define tribal tourism today.

· · ·

In the course of this endeavor I would like to thank Henry and Helen Coppinger, Jr., Alan W. Davis, Phil James; a very special thanks to W. Stanley and Mary Ellen Hanson, Jr., Thomas Carter, Juanita Cypress Osceola, Nellie Campbell, Ruth Holloway, Sara Lindsey, L. Mike Osceola, Ethel Freeman West; Jane Schryer, Mike Schryer, the family of O. B. Osceola, Sr., Jimmie O. Osceola, Virginia Roop Redman, Pete Osceola, Sr., Laura Mae Osceola, Mary Jane Cypress Storm, James E. Billie, Alan Jumper, Mary Tiger, Lena Cypress, Betty Cypress, Betty Mae Jumper, Dan Osceola, Howard Osceola, Bobby Henry, Suzie J. Billie, Carol Frank Cypress; Virginia M. Mitchell, Andy Buster, Mary Jean Koenes, Mary F. Johns; Rebecca A. Smith and Dawn Hugh, Historical Museum of Southern Florida, Miami; Sam Boldrick, Miami-Dade Public Library; Stuart McIver, Ft. Lauderdale; Donald Peyton, Dallas Historical Society; Billy L. Cypress and David M. Blackard, Ah-Tah-Thi-Ki Museum, Seminole Tribe of Florida, Hollywood; Jane Przybysz, McKissick Museum, Columbia, S.C.; George F. Boyer, Wildwood Historical Society, Wildwood, N.J.; and Cathy Creek, National Anthropological Archives, Smithsonian Institution, Washington, D.C. For technical services I thank William Freeman, K. C. and Ada Gannaway, Thelma P. Peters, Robert Webster, Chuck Buie, Daniel Rubin, Alexander Rubin, Susan Gillis, Linda H. Bair, Amy Faircloth, and, again, David M. Blackard. This work could not have been accomplished without the prior research of William C. Sturtevant, Harry A. Kersey, R. Thomas King, and James Covington and the availability of invaluable resource materials in the private and public papers of W. Stanley Hanson, Sr., Deaconess Harriet M. Bedell, and Ethel Cutler Freeman. For most recent contributions and insight I include anthropologist Jessica R. Cattelino and journalist Peter B. Gallagher.

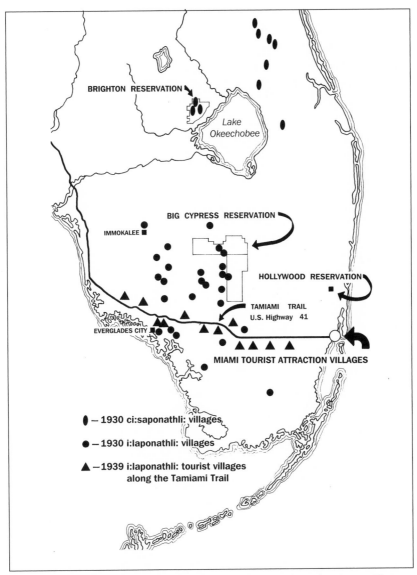

BRIGHTON RESERVATION

Lake Okeechobee

BIG CYPRESS RESERVATION

IMMOKALEE

HOLLYWOOD RESERVATION

TAMIAMI TRAIL
U.S. Highway 41

EVERGLADES CITY

MIAMI TOURIST ATTRACTION VILLAGES

● — 1930 ci:saponathli: villages

● — 1930 i:laponathli: villages

▲ — 1939 i:laponathli: tourist villages
along the Tamiami Trail

2. A map of southern Florida showing the city of Miami where the *i:laponathli:* went for tourist attraction employment as early as 1917, the location of *ci:saponathli:* and *i:laponathli:* villages in 1930 (based on Nash 1931), and the location of *i:laponathli:* tourist attraction villages along the Tamiami Trail in 1939 (based on Freeman 1939c). By David M. Blackard.

All Florida Indians from the tip of Florida to the north of Lake Okeechobee were popularly known as Florida Seminoles. Because Miami became
the major tourist mecca in southern Florida, it was the southernmost
group of them, the *i:laponathli:*, who first became immersed in the tourist
economy.

For most readers, *i:laponathli:* is a new term. With the Native Voice
gradually coming to be heard, it is important to acknowledge the self-
identity of tribal peoples, often quickly passed over—or not even mentioned by them—in past scholastic inquiries. (Sturtevant identified the
i:laponki: and *ci.saponki:* languages in 1971 [112].) In this book, it is of
foremost importance to identify the group responsible for creating and
participating in the unique tourist economy that brought forth important
cultural identifiers seen in today's Florida Indian culture.

The *i.laponki:* have been identified by the anthropological community
as *Mikasuki* speakers, *Mikasuki*-speaking Seminoles, or Mikasuki Seminoles, whose antecedents established themselves in Florida as early as
1740. Mikasuki (in many different spellings, including Miccosukee) referred originally to the large late-eighteenth-century town east of Tallahassee in northwest Florida, where the forebears of these people lived.

At that time the towns of the southeastern Indians had names, and the inhabitants were usually identified by the name of their town. In 1818, Andrew Jackson's forces made an illicit raid into northern Florida, destroying Seminole settlements, including the town of Mikasuki. Often, if the inhabitants moved a town, they kept the same name for solidarity (New Mikasuki was established in northern Florida), but as other refugees from Mikasuki fled into southern Florida no documentation shows that they regrouped into a town called Mikasuki (Cline 1974).

During the ensuing Second Seminole War (1835–42) and the Third (1855–58), however, the Mikasuki retained an important identity. Their warriors acquired a reputation as fierce, undaunted fighters, and their leaders fought tenaciously for their freedom to remain in Florida.

In Florida after the Seminole wars, the Mikasuki, who constituted about two-thirds of Florida's Indian population, and a smaller number of *Muscogee*-speaking Creeks (many of whom had arrived in Florida after their defeat in the Red Stick War of 1813–14), came to be generically called the "Florida Seminoles." In postwar days their identification in the literature would refer to the general region in which they lived or to waterways and towns near their major settlements, some of which were named after the Big Cypress Swamp, Cow Creek, Fish Eating Creek, Cat Fish Lake, and the Miami River.

In the twentieth century, the alteration of the eastern Everglades by drainage and improvements began. Settlers poured into the area. The *i:laponathli:*, whose daily life was in turmoil, needed to find a new economy. The development of a tourist economy came about spontaneously through unique relationships that had developed between the Indians and trusted non-Indian friends. The success of the endeavor was fired by the *i:laponathli:'* desire to retain their freedom, economic and otherwise, from the federal government. It was important politically to the *i:laponathli:* that their non-Indian friends kept them informed of government issues that might affect them. Significant non-Indians were allowed to represent the *i:laponathli:'* traditional tribal council formally. They presented the council's rulings directly to the media or to Washington. These two aspects, a long-term means of economic independence and the ability to have formal communication as an independent entity with the U.S. government, contributed to their retention of native tribal sovereignty.

Government programs, including the creation of federal reservations, became more active in the early twentieth century. The identity of the Florida Seminoles is important here because the majority of the non-reservation Indians—both *i:laponathli:* and *ci:saponathli:*—were adamantly antigovernment. The government had no official contact with these people for the first three decades of the twentieth century, yet officials felt compelled to create programs for the elusive Florida Seminoles. Significantly, beginning in the late 1920s, the *i:laponathli:* council began formally to dispute the government's right to act in their behalf. Through this process council members again strengthened their own concepts of sovereign rights.

The *i:laponathli:* called themselves Miccosukee when a portion of this group needed an identity for their tribal movement that culminated in the late 1960s. The nonpolitical name by which all of the *Mikasuki*-speakers called themselves was *i:laposhni: cha thli:* or the contraction *i:laponathli:* (singular: *i:laponi:*). They call their language *i:laponki:*. Phonetically *i:laponathli:* has a silent "l" and is pronounced: "i:laponathi:" (Sturtevant 1971: 112, 1997; Buster 1996a, b; Osceola 1996b, c; Billy L. Cypress 1996).

The *i:laponathli:* in turn call the minority population of *Muscogee*-speaking Creeks *ci.saposhni. cha thi* or *ci:saponathli:* (pronounced "ci:saponathi:") and their language *ci:saponki:*. The smaller *ci:saponathli:* population resided in prairies north of Lake Okeechobee and around its northeast shore. Both the *i:laponathli:* and *ci:saponathli:* had been participants in the hunting economy in the decades from 1870 to 1930 (Kersey 1975).

It was the *i:laponathli:'* emergence into the tourist market that "invented" this unique economy in which their culture itself became saleable. Tourism, it will be seen, more than any other endeavor, set the stage for the *i:laponathli:* to mold their identity and, with it, the popular conception of the Florida Seminoles. Activities were promoted that became long-term commercial ventures, and cultural symbols were created that permeated a society that remains "unconquered." *The Enduring Seminoles: From Alligator Wrestling to Ecotourism* is the legacy of the *i:laponathli:*.

CHAPTER 1

The End of an Era

The Everglades became small.

Sam Huff

At the close of the Third Seminole War in 1858, the *i:laponathli:* were no longer a desperate, hunted people. They were free to range over the Everglades in their trim cypress dugout canoes, hunting manatees and other aquatic animals in the bays and rivers. They raised cattle in the Big Cypress and found deer plentiful in the Big and Little Hunting Grounds south of the Miami River. With the lifting of the blockade of Florida at the end of the Civil War, they experienced an economic upswing as they hunted otters, deer, raccoons, and alligators for an international hide market and sought out rookeries of Everglades birds for the lucrative millinery trade (Kersey 1975).

In this matriarchal society, the women maintained droves of hogs and manufactured the native starch *coonti*. They sold the excess of both commodities to area settlers and in markets as far away as Key West. The *i:laponathli:* living on the southeastern coast actively engaged in salvaging materials and foodstuffs on the Atlantic beaches from the numerous wrecked ships or jettisoned cargos that were seasonal weather casualties of Gulf Stream shipping lanes (West 1985:6–7, 1992b:366).

The interior of the vast Everglades was gradually explored by surveyors who marveled that there were only inches of water covering innumerable acres of tillable soil. Many speculated on the feasibility of an engineering effort to drain this inland sea. The first active movement toward the reclamation of Florida's swamplands occurred in the 1880s. Hamilton Disston and the Trustees of the Internal Improvement Fund were the first developers to alter the southern Florida environment by building canals to connect many of the lakes in the upper Kissimmee Valley, north of Lake Okeechobee. This action had a significant effect on the water table, reclaiming some two million acres.

Minnie Moore Willson of Kissimmee became an early activist when she realized the plight of the Florida Seminoles, hoping to alert the country to the dim future she saw for these soon-to-be displaced Native Americans. In the second edition of her popular *Seminoles of Florida*, she wrote poetically of the threat of drainage to the northern *ci:saponathli:* as she had witnessed it from the Disston enterprise: "Dynamite blasts shake the very pans and kettles hanging around the wigwams and, while this monster of a machine destroys the only home of the tribe, is the time not ripe for decisive action in the protection of these wards of Florida?" (Willson 1910:134).

An elderly *ci.saponi:* identified as Pete Tiger related in 1956 how this drainage program had affected his environment and folkways: "In the old times we could paddle our canoes for many days and hunt the deer and the alligator. Now the white man has drained the Glades with his canals to make fields for his tomatoes and sugarcane. Our canoes cannot run on the sand and it is forbidden to cross the white man's fences. And the deer and the alligator each day go farther away" (Burman 1956:149).

The Disston experiment would have a major effect on the southern *i:laponathli:* because it proved beyond a doubt that the Florida Everglades could be drained. Governor Napoleon B. Broward took up the challenge. Work began at Fort Lauderdale in 1906 as a dredge began its march west-northwest from New River to Lake Okeechobee. Water was then channeled into canals where the level was controlled by locks. Additional canals were dug to drain the lake through rivers at Palm Beach, Deerfield, and Miami.

I:laponi: Sam Huff (Big Towns Clan) was born around 1872 in the Everglades on Pine Island, one of the earliest settlement islands documented in the eastern Everglades. (It is west of present-day Fort Lauderdale, near the outlet to New River.) Huff related the saga of the major Everglades drainage project from the *i:laponathli:* point of view in a poignant interview with anthropologist William C. Sturtevant in 1952: "Steam shovels began to make canals in the Everglades. Steam shovels came out of Fort Lauderdale and others came out of Deerfield, heading for Okeechobee. 'Just as soon as they hit the lake, the water is going to dry up in those Everglades, and as soon as the water dries up, they're going to start plantations'—that's what the white people said to the Indians. Another steam shovel went from Dania, and another one from Miami. Just as soon as they hit Okeechobee, the water was going to dry up. But I didn't believe it, until they hit Okeechobee. Then the water dried up, and even in Okeechobee it was dry too. The Everglades became small, and the trees grew very fast" (Sturtevant 1956:57, 65).

As both Pete Tiger and Sam Huff corroborate, the effects of drainage were immediate and disastrous to the life-style of the Florida Indians. The *i:laponathli:* who lived on the eastern seaboard south of the lake where many of their seasonal activities took place were greatly affected. Their hunting, gathering, and visiting patterns, their maritime skills, and innumerable other folkways were soon curtailed, altered, or lost for all time.

In the 1890s, government aid programs and organizations such as the Friends of the Florida Seminole, which was begun by Willson in 1899, attempted to locate land on which they hoped to persuade both the Creek and Mikasuki bands to settle permanently. But the *i:laponathli:* were not interested in anything with the government's stamp on it. Furthermore, their religious convictions were at odds with the concept of "owning" a piece of land. Like most Native Americans, they felt that the land belonged to everyone. Utilizing a single piece of land was also inconceivable, as it was contrary to the needs of their hunting and gathering economy. These cross-cultural ideological conflicts were the source of the nation's "Indian problem" which non-Indians saw saved through the natives' civilization and assimilation. They considered the Native Americans' only hope for survival in their becoming sedentary agriculturalists, forgoing their traditional tribalism in order to till the land and thus become "civilized" and accepted by mainstream America.

In 1892, the government attempted to set up an industrial camp in the Big Cypress that would teach the Florida Seminoles to live in a sedentary way. A sawmill and a farm were established, but the project failed because there was little native participation and many physical setbacks, such as a major fire (Kersey 1974:44–48).

The job of obtaining land for the Florida Seminoles had become a primary directive for the Seminole agent by 1894. Half of the appropriation for the industrial project was then earmarked for selecting and purchasing land on which to settle them. As Agent J. E. Brecht searched for suitable land, he took some settlers in the Miami area to court because they had applied for homesteads on land that should have been restricted by the state for the Florida Seminoles. In one case, Brecht regained the land, but the nonconfrontational *i:laponathli:* families who had been evicted never resettled the area (U.S. Cong., Exec. Doc., 1897:126; U.S. Cong. House, 1897:ccvi, ccxiii).

Henry Flagler, the Standard Oil magnate, brought his Florida East Coast Railroad south to Miami in 1896, and with it came a wave of settlers and investors and an even greater threat to the *i:laponathli:* way of life. In 1898, A. J. Duncan, U.S. Indian inspector, was sent to locate land on which to settle the Seminoles. With the aid of land surveyor J. O. Fries, who knew the locations of their settlements well, Duncan selected prime locations that had seen intensive settlement over the century. One was Pine Island, Sam Huff's birthplace, a complex of three settlement islands that had contained the significant postwar *i:laponathli:* survivors (as well as a handful of *ci:saponathli:*). All of them had been followers of the *i:laponi:* spiritual leader Sam Jones, *Abiaki* (Panther) (West 1989). The settlement history at the Pine Island complex was important to Duncan, who wanted to establish the Florida Seminoles' firm "right of occupancy" to this property.

Unfortunately, the islands were of odd configurations. They did not match the state's definition of swamplands, which dictated that in order to be declared swamplands—which could be transferred cheaply to the government—the landmass had to include an area covering a quarter-quarter section of a township. Duncan realized that the shape of the thin, irregular islands might pose a problem, and he called attention to the fact in his exhaustive report (U.S. Cong., House, 1898:ccxxxiv). However, in the final process, no special consideration was given to Duncan's wishes or to the historic significance of the islands, and only small, unusable portions of two of the islands had qualified. These bits and pieces actually became designated "Indian lands." One of the islands was more massive, and those usable parcels on Big City Island would be the nucleus of the Dania (now Hollywood) Reservation, which opened in 1926.

It was doubtful that the Florida Seminole population would have continued to remain in the areas that Duncan selected with such care. But it was not until 1911 that the lands formally became designated Indian lands by executive order. By that time they had been abandoned for a decade.

Subsistence problems as well as the encroachment of settlers seem to have compelled the Pine Island families to break into nuclear family groups to survive. Refugees from Miami's *i:laponathli:* settlements to the south of Pine Island had fled north to the island complex from the Snake Creek area around the period 1892–1900. This influx was reflected in a Seminole census for 1900 made by J. O. Fries: it showed more inhabitants "than people expected or believed" in the three-island complex. Some Pine Island refugees sought economic opportunities near the cities on the eastern coastal ridge, where they picked crops; others fled to smaller islands in the lower Everglades interior to continue their hunting and farming economy (Kersey 1981:155; West 1989:54).

In 1910, Indian Inspector Lorenzo D. Creel was engaged by the U.S. Government to survey the conditions of the Florida Seminoles. He found "no want" among them and described them as "satisfied, happy and content with their mode of life and . . . unanimously in favor of continuing therein." Yet "they are already decreasing in numbers and doomed ultimately to extinction," as shown by the high incidences of infant mortality and the probable increase of malarial disease. He added that because of their strong antigovernment attitude, their isolation, and the mobility of their communities, the establishment of an agency or attempts to provide education or "other civilizing agencies" would be "not only useless and impractical at this time, but an absolute waste of public money" (Creel 1911:36).

Creel did recommend that the lands obtained for the Seminole in 1911 should be kept for them for the future. He and former trading post operator Frank Stranahan of Fort Lauderdale told a group of nearby *i:laponathli:* that Washington had saved this land for them to live on, and "they could also have papers to show that the land was theirs as white men did." The elderly Charlie Osceola's answer to Creel's proposal shows a perspective on the Seminoles' fears about past wartime experiences. Osceola told Creel that he knew all about the Pine Island area and that it was good land, but "there is a big canal out there, pretty soon big steamboat came along put Injun on, *hiepus* [go] and never come back." He said how, when he was a little boy, he saw from his hiding place the soldiers get a lot of his people on a big steamboat, "*hiepus*, and never come back" (ibid.:15, 21).

In fact, the North and South New River drainage canals did landlock the Pine Island settlements. Charlie Osceola (Panther), born in 1843 (Seminole Agency 1977:77), had actually been a witness to this removal following the Third Seminole War. Reinforced from eyewitness accounts such as his, the younger generation of Seminoles developed a mindset against non-Indians that would be with the Florida Seminoles throughout much of the early twentieth century.

While Creel had recommended against the feasibility of hiring a special agent for the Florida Seminoles, conditions in south Florida became critical for the *i:laponathli:*. In 1912 the tanneries stopped purchasing alligator hides, a source of about 75 percent of the Indians' annual income. When the government realized their plight, Lucien A. Spencer was hired as special commissioner for the Florida Seminoles. He had his headquarters in Miami so as to be near them as they faced this economic crisis. Spencer noted in 1915 that "Were it not for the loss of the fur market caused by the European War they could easily secure money enough to make their necessary purchases of calico and coffee" (U.S. Department of the Interior 1915:1).

One of Spencer's first recommendations—a good one—was that "a tract of five or ten acres could be secured on the Miami River" where they would be close to Miami doctors (ibid. 1913:7). Locating the Seminole Agency in Miami would have made relations between the agency and the *i:laponathli:* more routine and would have made for better long-term relations, but nothing came of it. At his new post, Spencer was taken aback by the contrast of the Seminoles and Miami's inhabitants. "It is rather startling when we stop to think that within 200 miles of a city of at least 40,000 population there is a people, savage or at least semibarbarous, speaking a distinct language and utterly different in manner, dress, and customs from any other people in the world" (Spencer 1913:3).

. . .

How astounding, then, that in the near future such "semibarbarous" and reticent people would acquiesce to become featured attractions in Miami tourist enterprises, to suffer the "ignominy" of being stared at, to go about their traditional daily tasks under the gaze of strangers. Yet, however difficult it may have been for the *i:laponathli:* matriarchs to reach the decision to participate in the new economy of tourism, a significant number were moved to do so. By 1930, well over half the *i:laponathli:* population, even those in the isolated Big Cypress and in Collier County, had become involved in tourist attraction employment, while virtually all of the population was engaged in supplying goods to this novel market. A new economic era had begun.

CHAPTER 2

The Beginnings of an Industry

It's June in Miami.

Electric sign, Broadway and 42nd St., New York City, winter, 1920s

The Miami River flowed only four and a half miles out of the Everglades before reaching Biscayne Bay. In the days before drainage, the Miami River Rapids fell six feet over a course of four hundred to five hundred feet. During the rainy season, the water over the falls had a velocity of fifteen miles per hour. This natural phenomenon has been described as "a scene of enchantment" (Smiley 1968). Along this river the town of Miami was incorporated in 1896.

That year, Flagler opened the fabulous Royal Palm Hotel at the mouth of the Miami River, at the terminus of his Florida East Coast Railroad. Guests from the hotel took small excursion boats such as the popular *Sallie* upriver to Richardson's Citrus Grove. The tourists disembarked amid fragrant fruit trees and strolled down sun-filled lanes, sipping fruit punch and doubtless thinking of relatives and friends back home in dreary, cold, snow-covered cities.

The grove was located on an island between the north and south forks of the river. The A. J. Richardson family had settled there in 1897. The island came to be called Musa Isle, after the botanical name for the bananas that grew there in great luxuriance. In addition to grove fruit, the Richardsons sold tropical jams, jellies, and marmalades and formally called their business Musa Isle Fruit Farm (*Miami News* 1962; Redman 1981).

Another early, rather rude riverside attraction, operated by Warren Frazee, was located on Wagner Creek near downtown Miami. Frazee, popularly known as "Alligator Joe," had had exploits with the saurians that were a source of local news. Around 1910, he dammed up a natural slough on Wagner Creek and installed an attraction featuring alligators. He had made a name for himself with a similar attraction in Palm Beach in 1895 and likewise entertained early tourists in Fort Lauderdale in 1897 (*Tropical Sun* 1895; Stout Papers; Coppinger 1975). His Miami venture appears to have been an instant success. The alligator farm was a bona fide tourist attraction by 1911 when it became part of the Biscayne Navigation Company's sightseeing boat tours.

Joe was not a passive showman. He got into the pens with the saurians and appears to have been the first person who could be considered a "professional" alligator wrestler. The *Miami Herald* enthusiastically stated, "His manipulation of the gators and crocs is the cause of much wonder. More visitors see Joe's performances in Florida each winter than go to any other single attraction" (1911b).

The *i:laponathli:* who came into Miami from the Everglades traveled down Wagner Creek, especially when conditions were such that they could not navigate the rapids. In 1911, a Seminole camp was noted "near the alligator farm" (*Miami Herald* 1911a). In December 1915 thirty *i:laponathli:* were camped "on the banks of the Miami River near the alligator farm" (*Miami Metropolis* 1915a). The alligator farm was owned by L. C. Rook, J. C. Twiggen, and E. E. Rhine and managed by "Buck Hamilton, who is responsible for the success of Alligator Joe" (ibid. 1915b). A festivity was planned at the Seminole camp on Christmas and during the following week. This rather tenuous joint "attraction" created by the alligator farm and the Indian camp about two blocks away is probably the earliest documented forerunner of the *i:laponathli:'* long-term relationship with tourism.

The excursion boats brought tourists to these outlying river attractions, making continuous daily runs upriver as far as the rapids. A land speculation company created another attraction at this terminus: a wooden tower, twenty-five feet high, on the edge of the Everglades. Tourists left the boats and took a rail cart pulled by a mule through willow and myrtle thickets to the site, then paid ten cents to climb to the top. There they could see the vast expanse of water and little islands, which they were told would soon be dry land as a result of the efforts of the Drainage Commission.

Richardson sold his interest in Musa Isle in 1907 to John A. Roop from Missouri. Roop continued the development of the grove by specializing in mail orders, but visitors were still vital to the business. Some of the grove's most distinguished patrons were the Mellons and Roosevelts, who arrived at the Musa Isle dock in their private yachts. The grove's popularity grew, and it became famous for serving Musa Isle Punch, made from five varieties of fruit. The Royal Palm Hotel purchased it to serve in their fine dining room. But the end was in sight for Musa Isle Grove: As the drainage programs escalated in the Miami area and the Miami Canal opened into the Miami River in 1909, the trees withered for lack of water (Redman 1981).

Meanwhile, on the south fork of the river, around the bend of the island, horticulturist and landscape designer Henry Coppinger, Sr., purchased ten acres and built a home in 1911. An immigrant from Cork, Ireland, Coppinger came to Miami from central Florida following the disastrous freezes of 1894–95. In 1897, he was in charge of landscaping the Royal Palm Hotel and Flagler's Bahamian hotels, the Colonial and the Royal Victoria in Nassau (*Miami Herald* 1922a; Coppinger 1975). He began to plant exotic foliage alongside the lush native vegetation in the Coppinger hammock property, which soon became known as Coppinger's Tropical Gardens.

Coppinger continued to import ornamental plants and sold them from his nursery. Many of his rare specimens are now commonplace in south Florida yards: the single and double hibiscus, the white poinsettia, the ti plant, and the *Monsteria deliciosa*. Noted botanist Dr. David Fairchild (who later established the internationally acclaimed Fairchild Tropical Garden in south Miami) was a frequent visitor, bringing his friends to see the rare vegetation Coppinger had imported (*Miami Herald* 1922a; James 1980).

In 1915 an aggressive newspaper and magazine advertising campaign was mounted to sell Miami as a mecca for tourists and investors, as a land of opportunity. The advertising strategy must have worked, as Miami was growing rapidly. Around 1915, a rivalry began that would continue for decades between Coppinger's Tropical Gardens and Musa Isle Grove.

A new tour boat was forced away from the Musa Isle dock by an established rival. The concessioner looked for a place he could take his party and found it at Coppinger's landing. New in the business, he could not afford to pay the Coppingers, but he suggested that the family charge the tourists for a tour of the garden and sell fruit punch. The Coppinger family's punch contained *seven* fruits, two more than Musa Isle's (Coppinger 1975; James 1980).

While Alligator Joe may have premiered the alligator as an attraction feature, the person who made the term *alligator wrestling* a household word was Henry Coppinger, Jr. Born on the Miami River in 1898, young Henry had amused himself by stalking and catching baby alligators. He would stuff them inside his shirt and sell them for fifteen cents each to the Greeks who ran curio shops in town. As he grew older, he would dive into the river to retrieve three to four footers. When the tourists began to arrive at his father's attraction, Henry caught an alligator and penned it up in a slough on the riverfront. The news traveled, and a busload of tourists arrived just to see young Henry's alligator (Coppinger 1975).

As enterprising tourist attractions and investors in this burgeoning subtropical city reached toward prosperity, economic conditions worsened for the *i:laponathli:*. Their settlements and farms on the east coast were gradually confiscated by investors who gained legal title to the property. By 1917, Indian families in the Fort Lauderdale area under widowed matriarch Annie Jumper Tommie (Panther) began to pick crops for white farmers, often on land that they had once farmed themselves (West 1985:9).

Annie's mother, Mammy Jumper, was a *ci:saponi:* (Panther clan). Her family consisted of the handful of Creek-speakers who had resided in the postwar *i:laponathli:* enclave at the Pine Island complex. An observer wrote of them in 1918, "[These Indians] living near Fort Lauderdale are somewhat more progressive than some of the others. They have been forced by circumstances to seek employment and occasionally work on the truck farms there and at Miami, and it is said that they make fairly good laborers. But most of the tribe still look upon such employment with haughty disdain" (Winter 1918:142). Indeed, the *i:laponathli:* considered this family different and therefore a threat to the *i:laponathli:'* traditional way of life.

Meanwhile, drainage programs had curtailed *i:laponathli:* trade in the Miami area. Miami's last major frontier trading post, Girtman Brothers, had closed in 1915, citing as a major reason the effects of the drainage program that cut off water routes and made it impossible for the Indians to get their peltry to the post (Comstock 1938:12).

Coppinger's Tropical Gardens formally opened to the public in time for the tourist season of 1917. A disastrous February freeze hit a few weeks later, and temperatures dropped to 27 degrees for two mornings in a row. According to the Weather Bureau, it was the lowest temperature ever recorded in Miami (*Miami Herald* 1917a). The succulent tropical plantings in the garden were destroyed.

Henry, Jr., related how the first Seminole camp was established at the gardens that year. Construction of the Tamiami Trail, the first trans-Everglades highway, had begun in Miami. The driver of a Miami tour bus located an Indian camp on the construction bed just outside the city. The tourists got out, looked over the camp, and had their photos made with the Indians. It was great for business, but one day when he arrived the Indians were gone. The tourists demanded their money back. The guide came to the Coppinger family and suggested that if they would add a Seminole camp as a feature of the garden, he would provide busloads of tourists (Smiley 1967).

The area *i:laponathli:* were familiar with the Coppinger property, having camped there as late as 1898 (Willoughby 1898:44). Perhaps they had sought the warmth of the Miami River for their winter camp. Phil James, an employee at the attraction from 1918 to 1922, noted that it was the 1917 freeze that he believed had brought the Indians to the Coppingers' site (James 1980).

Money, rations, cloth, and warmth were incentives for the family of Jack Tiger Tail to return to Coppinger's attraction from their Everglades camp twenty-five miles west of Homestead (*Miami Herald* 1917b). Jack Tiger Tail was Wind Clan, his wife Big Towns. By 1918, the Tiger Tails were residing at Coppinger's for the brief but significant tourist season, January 1 to April 30. Tiger Tail was a popular figure in Miami. He spoke English fairly well and probably could read and write like his brother Charlie. Tiger Tail was very visible and involved himself in local affairs. In 1917, he headed a search team looking for a lost surveying party in the Everglades (ibid., 1917b, 1922e).

Obviously based on the Coppingers' success, by 1919 John Roop appears to have compensated for his damaged grove by leasing a portion of the Musa Isle property west of the Roop home to the first *i:laponi:* entrepreneur, Willie Willie (Bird Clan). Willie Willie established the Musa Isle Trading Post along with the Seminole Village. The post was utilized by white trappers as well, providing yet another attraction for Musa Isle's tourists: seeing the hunters come in from the Everglades with their bounty. It was estimated that by 1930 hunting still constituted two-thirds of the Seminoles' income (Nash 1931:37). *I:laponathli:* families who came to trade at the post stayed three or four days and brought all of their livestock with them—dogs, chickens, and hogs. To supplement the camp's supply of commercial food, the men often went hunting and brought back fresh meat. The women periodically gathered the native starch plant *coonti*, which grew in the pinelands near the attractions. These traditional foods were processed and prepared at the attraction camps and added to the atmosphere of the frontier and the Indian experience (Davis 1980).

Willie and his father, Charlie Willie (Big Towns), also had a trading establishment in the Everglades west of Miami. The Willies bought the Indians' hides at that location and shipped them in to Willie Willie's Musa Isle Post. There they sold directly to the market, eliminating the usual non-Indian middleman and making a huge profit (Coppinger 1975; James 1980; Osceola 1982).

Pluming had been a major source of *i:laponathli:* income in the late nineteenth century, but in 1900, through the efforts of the National Audubon Society, plume hunting had been outlawed by federal law. Yet, in the early twentieth century, bird plumage was still in great demand for ornamentation on ladies' hats. The *i:laponathli:* had made a lucrative income from the many bird rookeries in the Everglades and continued to do so—illegally—well into the twentieth century.

As Kersey noted, hunting for plumage "persisted well into the 1920s because of the demands of fashion; and it was only the change in women's tastes that brought it to an end, not the Audubon Society or the law. A single egret plume could bring as much as five to ten dollars in the illicit market, or up to thirty-two dollars an ounce—roughly the plumes of four birds." In May 1919, while at Musa Isle, Willie Willie was arrested along with a non-Indian for violating the "Migratory Bird Treaty Between Great Britain and the United States." Willie and his partner had between them $7,000 worth of bird plumage (Kersey 1975:76, 81).

Willie Willie was unique in his own culture, not only as a businessman but in other acculturated ways as well. He seemed equally at home in the non-Indian community, where he dressed in the latest fashion, as a mannequin for Burdine's, Miami's major department store. He was also married to a non-Indian, a practice unheard of in those days and one in disfavor with both cultures.

One insider estimated that Willie Willie's various business interests at Musa Isle cleared $50,000 annually. "[He] had more money than he could use. He married outside his tribe and burned up the highways in his high priced car" (Glenn 1982:81). However, Alan W. Davis, a hunter who became the foreman of the Musa Isle Indian Village, and Lucien A. Spencer, the special commissioner of the Seminole Agency, identified the sale of egret plumes as the business in which Willie Willie made his real money (Davis 1980; U.S. Department of the Interior 1919:9–10).

During the boom years of the 1920s, a large "electric" sign in the heart of New York City at Broadway and 42nd Street glowed warmly in the cold of January, proclaiming, "It's June in Miami!" (Bellamy 1980:2). A similar sign in Hot Springs, Arkansas, read, "A piece of Florida is a piece of Gold" (deVane 1978:193). Tourists and investors flocked to Miami.

At Coppinger's, young Henry was able to aid his father's damaged gardens and recoup some of the lost tourist trade. After his success with one alligator on display, he collected fifteen more. Soon he had a hundred, from gnarled ancients to hatchlings. He created his own concession at the garden, calling it the "Alligator Farm," but it too suffered a setback because of competition with Musa Isle. The *Eagle Magazine* noted, "Just before the new farm was scheduled to open its gates, a neighbor, with more enterprise than business ethics, suddenly stocked his own place which was nearer the highway . . . with all sizes of alligators, and out front erected a big sign, 'Alligator Farm'" (1929:10).

The Coppinger family tried to buy out Musa Isle's alligator interests but failed (James 1980, 1981). However, Henry found a way to beat the competition temporarily. He had noted how excited the tourists became when he entered the alligator pens, and, like Alligator Joe, he began to wrestle the saurians. The results of Henry's showmanship temporarily depleted Musa Isle of tourists as they flocked to Coppinger's Alligator Farm to see Henry Coppinger, billed as "The Alligator Boy" (Coppinger 1975; Smiley 1967). At a quarter a head admission to the garden and a quarter more to see Henry's alligator show, the attraction successfully recovered from the freeze, and Henry, Jr., established professional alligator wrestling as an enterprise that he popularized, with shows at large pools throughout the nation.

Meanwhile, at Musa Isle, Willie Willie had become aggressive in his business dealings. He precipitated a direct conflict with Coppinger around 1922 by erecting a signboard advertising Musa Isle on one of the entrance roads to Coppinger's Tropical Gardens. Henry countered by placing a larger sign advertising Coppinger's next to it. When the Coppinger sign was demolished. Henry accused Willie Willie, who came to Coppinger's in a temper, threatening Henry with a pistol (Coppinger 1975; James 1980).

Early in 1922, John Roop sold his failing grove to a developer, John A. Campbell. Upon taking possession of the property and getting ready to subdivide it for home sites, however, Campbell discovered that Egbert L. (Bert) Lasher held a lease to the prime waterfront property known as Musa Isle Indian Village (Redman 1981; Campbell 1981a). Both *i:laponathli:* and white sources close to the situation were told that Willie Willie had been induced to sign away whatever claim he had to Musa Isle, delivering the property into Bert Lasher's hands (Davis 1980; James 1980; Glenn 1982:100).

Kersey's information supports this theory. Willie Willie died of tuberculosis in June 1929. Elizabeth Willie Willie, his white wife, was dying in a New York hospital in 1930 when she brought charges against Lasher. She claimed that Lasher had taken Willie Willie's business without compensation. "Her claim was brought to the attention of Congresswoman Ruth Bryan Owen of Miami, who urged the office of Charles J. Rhodes, commissioner of the Bureau of Indian Affairs, to check into the matter. This move led to investigations by the Department of Justice and the Federal Bureau of Investigation, which unearthed a great deal of circumstantial evidence that Willie Willie was probably defrauded out of his business. However, since the alleged fraud had not taken place on an Indian reservation, an assistant U.S. attorney issued the opinion that it was not a federal offense and the case was closed" (Kersey 1989:44).

While Lasher has been described by a former employee as a born "promoter" with a "dynamic" personality (Carter 1981), his past was cloudy indeed. Prior to opening a small tourist attraction in Fort Lauderdale in 1921 and 1922 (an event in which Willie Willie also appeared as a key player), Lasher had been convicted of dealing in stolen cars and had served time in prison (Glenn 1982:81; McIver 1988).

Yet, while the competitive nature of Lasher's attraction business sometimes created incidents between *i:laponathli:* employees at Musa Isle and those at Coppinger's, interviews with former employees, *i:laponathli:* and non-Indian, have been positive and showed loyal support of Lasher's character. He was an alcoholic, however, and as a result his employees were sometimes inconvenienced and his businesses eventually failed. But for over two decades (1922–43), he appears to have had a unique influence in *i:laponathli:* politics and in support of their sovereignty rights. His attractions (Musa Isle, Osceola's Gardens, and Osceola Indian Village, all in Miami) were often locations for press conferences. He offered a firm resolve and backed the *i:laponathli:* in their stand against the government. He was responsible for introducing them to their long-time legal council, O. B. White (Davis 1980; West 1981:203).

The year 1922 was a lucrative season for both Musa Isle and Coppinger's. The latter had matured into a rare showplace of tropical vegetation. A full-page article in the *Miami Herald* featured "Coppinger's Pirate's Cove," as the attraction business was known by 1922. The landscape artistry of the senior Coppinger was praised, as were the novelties of the plant nursery and the Alligator Farm, where opportune tourists could see baby alligators hatch from eggs (*Miami Herald* 1922a).

Although Musa Isle continued to be called "Willie Willie's Indian Village" during the 1922 tourist season, the attraction was by then firmly in the hands of Bert and Martha Lasher. On January 29, a crowd of over 3,000 persons witnessed a "Seminole wedding," which was to become a Lasher trademark (*Miami Herald* 1922b). Not to be outdone, the Coppingers responded with weddings in their village.

The competition between Musa Isle and Coppinger's Pirate's Cove Indian Village not surprisingly caused friction between the *i:laponathli:* employees. Agent Lucien A. Spencer reported in 1925, "Rivalry between two Indian camps near Miami led the leaders of one camp to assault those of the other" (U.S. Department of the Interior, 1925:2).

Thus with their hide economy waning, the adaptable *i:laponathli:* involved themselves in a new economy, one in which they were encouraged to practice their traditional life-style and where they were an economic asset. A future special commissioner to the Seminoles, James L. Glenn, was prompted to note, "Their own private folkways have a cash value that must be bewildering" (Tebeau 1957:65).

CHAPTER 3

The Business of Hype

But it was worth all that to see!

Norma Davis, reporter

Miami's cultural contrast helped to make the *i:laponathli:* popular: the Florida natives contrasted nicely with the ultramodern Art Deco landscape. The *Hollywood Herald* reported in 1936, "Not thirty miles from the 'flesh pots' of southeastern Florida cities where white inhabitants live in luxury that no civilization has ever equaled, where streamlined automobiles and trains rocket over the earth and the drone of airplanes is regularly heard in the far reaches of the atmosphere over the earth, where in short men live that ultra-civilized life which is called the mark of the march of progress, there floats a dugout canoe. In the canoe is a man primeval whose father and whose father's father poled or paddled similar canoes."

By the 1930s, the Seminole villages at Miami and Silver Springs near Ocala had become the leading tourist businesses in the state. The *i:laponathli:* were sought after by local organizations and promoters who wished to engage these Native Americans in special events through their tourist attraction connections. Alan W. Davis of Musa Isle escorted delegations of *i:laponathli:* to countless openings and marched with them in many parades on Flagler Street. They were on hand to meet the first passenger ship from the Clyde Line on its inaugural trip to Miami in November 1929. *I:laponathli:* men took a ride over the Everglades on the Good Year dirigible *Defender* that December, and in a contrast of "primitive" and "modern" technology they were hired to paddle in their cypress dugout canoes in October 1931 to meet the *American Clipper,* a forty-passenger seaplane of the Pan American Airway System (West 1981:214). Children from the Seminole Village at Musa Isle were greeted by none other than Mickey Mouse in September 1934 (*Miami Herald* 1934). The "Seminoles," according to the media, "added color" to local events in their bright orange, yellow, pink, red, and light and dark blue patchwork clothing of the 1920s and 1930s.

As the *i:laponathli:* were making their impact on the Miami tourist attractions in the 1920s, a major promotion with a "Seminole" theme was created for the new town of Hialeah northwest of Miami. *Hialeah* means "high prairie" in the *i:laponki:* language. The new town was created on drained Everglades lands over which the *i:laponathli:* had not long before sailed their canoes on their way to trade in Miami. The land was developed by aircraft pioneer Glenn Curtis in partnership with cattle rancher James Bright.

The streets of the new town were given Seminole-sounding names. From as far away as Jacksonville, huge billboards, twenty to thirty feet high, showed Jack Tiger Tail, headman at Coppinger's, pointing the way to the new city (*Hialeah Home News* 1964). His gesturing likeness was taken as the town's logo. Buses transporting prospective buyers to Hialeah from Miami were painted in "Indian colors" of red, yellow, black, and white, the traditional Seminole medicine colors. The Hialeah Golf Course also employed some *i:laponathli:* as caddies. Stereotypically, they were considered "ideal" for this line of work, as they could follow the ball, due to their "marvelous eyesight trained for years in the impenetrable vastness of the Everglades" (Sessa 1951:24). Soon, and for decades thereafter, the *i:laponathli:* were associated with special high media and famous patron events at Hialeah Racetrack where they were hired to parade in the infield.

A 1922 photo shows a Hialeah bus sporting a large advertisement for "Willie Willie's Indian Village and Musa Isle Grove" (Fishbaugh 1922). When Willie Willie lost Musa Isle to Bert Lasher that year, he was encouraged by the founders of Hialeah to set up another Indian Village in Hialeah's "Sport Section" at Palm Avenue and 19th Street, a location catering to patrons of the racetrack. His attraction was popular and continued to feature a trading post for hides. A tourist magazine, *Happenings in Miami*, advised in 1925, "See this by all means!"

The City of Miami actively promoted both Coppinger's Pirate's Cove and Musa Isle Seminole Village by bringing notable guests to the attractions. Often a welcoming ceremony with the Seminoles was arranged for publicity.

At Musa Isle, Bert and Martha Lasher held a contest to name the first-born child of Musa Isle headman Cory Osceola (Big Towns) and his wife, Juanita Cypress Osceola (Panther). Of the many entries, Dorothy, meaning "Gift of God," was chosen. Their daughter was thus christened *Tahama*—in *i:laponki:* Gift of God—in a well-advertised celebration at the attraction on July 14, 1925 (*Miami Daily News* 1925). The *News* reported, "When the papoose was born the first Seminole to start life in a white man's hospital, her parents offered a $25 prize to the person suggesting the most appropriate name for her. Hundreds of letters from all over the country came to the *Daily News* and the Musa Isle Village and from the long lists of names Cora [*sic*] and Juanita chose Ta-Ha-Ma."

But the Lashers' most successful venture appeared to have been producing the popular Seminole weddings. Cory Osceola had been in residence at the attraction when Juanita Cypress's parents, Futch (Otter) and Ruby (Panther), arrived with their children from their camp in Collier County on the western side of the Everglades. Cory and Juanita were formally married at Musa Isle in 1923. One of their sons, O. B. White Osceola, Sr. (Panther), translated for his mother about their marriage ceremony in an interview in 1985. "Yeah, [they had] a celebration for them. When they do that, they advertised alot and they get alot of people in the village, alot of excitement. At the same time, they make alot of money too. That's part of the game."

A standing-room-only wedding took place between Musa Isle headman Tony M. B. Tommie (Panther) and Edna Johns (Big Towns) (both *ci:saponi:*) in June 1926. It was obviously scheduled to hold tourists in Miami until June. No wonder that the Seminole Village attractions were applauded by the Chamber of Commerce and city commissioners as assets to area tourism. The *Miami News* described the event, staged before a capacity crowd at Musa Isle: "They crashed delightedly through the huts in the Indian Village in the rush to get a good view of the ceremony. . . . They knocked over kettles and stepped in frying pans and were blithely happy. Some even climbed to the trembly palmetto thatched roofs of the pool shelters and stabbed their feet into the dry spread leaves. But it was worth all that to see" (Davis 1926).

The elder John Osceola (Panther) performed the ceremony. The crowd flung coins and bills at the bridal pair. The multitude of Miami residents, tourists, and media snacked on fry bread and coffee (Davis 1980). Dances from the annual religious activity, the Green Corn Dance, were led by Cory Osceola. Alligator wrestling contests, canoe racing, and archery contests rounded out the day (*Miami Herald* 1926a, b). (Some family members have questioned this marriage, but the Seminole Agency's Reconstructed Census Roll validates it [Seminole Agency 1977].)

There is no doubt that some of the couples participating in the wedding extravaganzas were already married, even with children, when their "vows" were witnessed at the tourist attractions. Reverend Glenn voiced his objections:

> This is neither Indian nor a wedding, and the people of Miami know it and even some of the tourists know it. One Indian boy was married so often that too many of the tourists came to remember that, "That's the boy they married off last year." Since the Indian girl is most attractive between the ages of fifteen and twenty, the "bride" must be taken from this age group, but the Indian boy is still in the gosling state until after he is twenty, so the "groom" must be considerably older. He often is a man with a wife and several children, but he is at his prime and is supposed to know enough acting to play this farce through to the end. As the time draws near the busses from downtown pour out excited and strange people from every part of the nation, and from every social strata of life. The stage has been well set, the show is already going strong. The cash register sings its wildest symphony. The packed throngs wait in eagerness for the curtain to rise, only there is no curtain. The "medicine man," who here is acting, leads [this] riotously dressed Indian man and girl before the crowd. In the name of matrimony he invokes a solemn pledge from each, only the girl may be giggling in the meantime. And then to ascend to the seventh heaven of pure, undiluted farce the "groom" wraps his arm about the "bride" and plants a pair of saliva coated lips on her face. They both shudder, and she grabs her dress or cape and wipes away the residue of this filthy habit. The

gifts from the stores of Miami are handed over to the "new bride and groom," and for days the Indians chuckle over what fools these tourists really are. They also wonder about that something man has called *Fraud*. The more thoughtful say, "May be so alright for white man, no good for Indian." (Glenn 1982:102, 104)

But the lucrative economy earned from the Miami villages would soon be in jeopardy. In September 1926 the worst hurricane Miamians had witnessed bore down on south Florida. Its force was so great that it devastated southeastern Florida, sending the area from boom-time prosperity toward the bust of the depression almost overnight. Willie Willie's Hialeah attraction was demolished. Musa Isle and Coppinger's were severely damaged. Alligators were loose, buildings were flooded, trees and vines were everywhere. Musa Isle repaired and reopened. Coppinger's hammock suffered its greatest damage from the tangle of vegetation, and the attraction was closed for two years (Downs 1981:227).

The main sources of transportation available for visitors to the riverside attractions continued to be the sightseeing boats, popular attractions in their own right. Both Seminole village attractions depended heavily on boat tours, especially in their early years of operation. Coppinger's was serviced by the double-decker sightseeing boat *Dixie* well into the 1940s. Musa Isle was serviced by the *Seminole Queen*. Barkers hawked tourists at Miami's Bayfront boat concessions, where Seminole women sat sewing as an advertisement.

On New River in Fort Lauderdale, the earliest of the famous *Jungle Queen* sightseeing boats was built by Captain Al Starts in 1935. It held fifty passengers. Following World War II, Starts asked Moses Jumper (Panther) and Betty Mae Jumper (Snake) of the nearby Dania (now Hollywood) Reservation to set up a small Seminole village on the New River where the tourists could see alligator wrestling and where families living on the reservation could sell crafts. In 1946 a 250-seat *Jungle Queen* was built, and business boomed. Many of the now middle-aged residents of Hollywood Reservation were children who sang "Jesus Loves Me" at the *Jungle Queen* Seminole Village and posed for tips from camera-toting tourists. "Doing the boats" on New River for the several tour boat concessions was just part of a day's activities for many children from the Hollywood Reservation (West 1987a).

Silver Springs Seminole Village near Ocala was operated by Charles H. Metzger. The attraction continued growing in popularity under herpetologist/showman Ross Allen. Early families who participated in this attraction were Big Cypress residents under headman Charlie Cypress (Otter), his wife Lee (Panther), Billy Homespun (Otter), and George Osceola (Deer). It was the most northern of the well-established Seminole Indian village attractions. When the Big Cypress group arrived for the November 1935 season, it was extremely cold. "My folks pretty cold. No got blanket!" George Osceola announced to Metzger. An advertisement appeared in the local paper: "Special announcement has been made by Mr. Metzger that on Thanksgiving Day any person will be admitted free to the village if they will bring a wrapped article that will contain some used clothing or covering for the Indians" (*Florida Digest* 1935). That season the *Tampa Tribune* (1935) announced, "Silver Springs wins claim as No. 1 Lure" in Florida with more than 500,000 visitors annually.

Ethel Cutler Freeman had an association with the Anthropology Department of the American Museum of Natural History, and she maintained an interest in the Florida Seminoles. An amateur anthropologist from Morristown, New Jersey, her general observations on the *i:laponathli:* tourist attractions have proven valuable. She reported in 1941 that the Silver Springs Village was "very large and is well run and clean" (Freeman 1941a).

By 1932, Coppinger's Pirate's Cove was operated by the elderly widow of Henry Coppinger, Sr. Freeman noted that Mrs. Coppinger did not want the place "cheaply commercial": "The Jungle gardens are extensive and after wandering around and through them for some time, one finds an almost hidden Seminole camp, quite isolated. It looks like a real village of their own." Freeman's assessment of Musa Isle was, in contrast, "This is absolutely a commercial camp. It is run to make money and it does no[t] pretend to be anything else. It is very large, and it is advertised on the circulars, in the guide books and hotels and tourist buses take sight seers to it. It is well managed, however, and clean. . . . Barkers stand around and yell, 'Guide just leaving to see the only Indians who have not acknowledged our Government'" (ibid.).

Lasher had proven to John A. and Nellie Campbell, owners of the Musa Isle property, that the Seminole Village was a lucrative asset. He had been operating under a lease from them since 1928, but in 1932 Lasher went bankrupt and lost Musa Isle after putting a decade of effort into the business and establishing it as a premier Miami attraction. Musa Isle continued to operate under the Campbells' management, then the George Staceys, Campbell's daughter and son-in-law (Campbell 1981a). Lasher then started anew, opening Osceola Gardens Indian Village (1933–35) nearby on the Miami Canal at 2700 N.W. 27th Avenue. Eleven *i:laponki:* families were living there in 1935 (*Miami Daily News* 1935). The Indian

Village was a new concession at an established attraction, Osceola Gardens, a dance hall and beer garden.

Lasher never recovered financially from his initial bankruptcy, doubtless because his alcoholism was growing worse and his health was failing as a result. The receiver for Osceola's Garden Indian Village in 1934 noted, "The beer garden has been furnishing Lasher with booze on demand, Lasher has been violent and foul mouthed and in a constant state of drunkenness" (Dade County Chancery Records 1934:5). The receiver entered into the chancery record on January 21, 1936, that, "Lasher has permitted and encouraged the Indians living upon the corporation premises to become intoxicated and raise disturbance upon the premises, calling for police intervention."

In 1937, Lasher opened yet another village, Osceola's Indian Village (1937–43) at N.W. 36th Street and River Drive on the Miami Canal, the canal that drained the Everglades through the Miami River. Freeman also described this attraction: "Of all the villages, this is the most harmful to the Indians. It is on a busy corner in the outskirts of Miami, near the Hialeah Racetrack. Outside of the enclosure are a number of the cheapest kinds of stores and booths, where they sell liquor, and nick nacks, and candies, pop, etc. Barkers stand outside and hail autos and call, 'This is the only Indian Village that contains 4 tribes of Indians'" (Freeman 1941a).

As might be expected, the popularity of Miami's Indian village attractions gave rise to smaller attractions around the state. In March 1937, "four carloads" of *ci:saponathli:* from Dania Reservation camped for four days at the St. Petersburg Recreation Pier. Ben Tommie (Panther), Robert (perhaps Richard) Osceola (Bird), and twenty-two others participated in this engagement with their pastor, Willie King, an Oklahoma Creek, who headed the Seminole Baptist Church on the Dania Reservation. E. G. Barnhill, who operated an "Indian trading post" on the pier, arranged for their participation. The pier planned to "make an enclosure of palms with thatched entrance, to give the setting the appearance of an Indian camp" (*St. Petersburg Times* 1937a, b; *St. Pete Independent* 1937). The next year Richard Osceola, a *ci:saponi:* (Bird), and two unidentified men, two women, and twelve children had set up a small attraction at Wild Bill's Zoo, thirty miles north of Palm Beach (*Miami Herald* 1938a). This attraction involved almost 10 percent of the *ci:saponathli:* population.

Former state archaeologist Vernon Lamme took his acquaintances, the family of Josie (Bear) and Pocahontas Huff Jumper (Panther) of the Dania Reservation, to Marineland Aquarium (south of St. Augustine) in 1941. Josie Jumper had been on an early exposition trip with *i:laponathli:* to

Canada in 1931. Lamme received a concession that featured an aboriginal burial mound located in a lot near the Marineland tourist attraction. The Jumpers were to construct their camp near the site and serve as a modern-day Indian continuum. They were allowed to sell their crafts. The Marineland Studios drew up strict regulations concerning their participation. According to Lamme's contract, he was "permitted to bring Josie Jumper and his family to Marineland, with the understanding that they would have to go immediately with the first complaint regarding their conduct, regarded by the Management as sufficient" (Tolstoy 1941).

In 1916, the annual Seminole Sun Dance festival was created at West Palm Beach with a Seminole theme. The festival was to encourage tourists to remain in the Palm Beaches after the traditional end of the season, which (in 1916) was Washington's birthday, February 22. Held in late March or early April, the festival hosted a parade that included Seminole and Ku Klux Klan participants (Byrons Studio 1916; Biggers 1936). The festival had been reorganized by the 1930s to feature a grand variety of activities from pet parades to gymkhanas. By 1936, the Seminole theme had been updated to reflect the Seminoles' "Unconquered" persona. The event's organizers saw the festival appealing to tourists "as it dramatizes the only tribe in the country that has not been subdued by federal arms" (*Palm Beach Post* 1936).

Not to be outdone by West Palm Beach, the Bok or "Singing" Tower attraction in Lake Wales hosted its own version of the Sun Dance. Forty-eight *i:laponathli:* (almost an eighth of the population) attended the 1936 festivities with W. Stanley Hanson. The group included the families of Charley Cypress, John Cypress, George Osceola, Jack Motlow, Little Charlie Billie, Ingraham Billie, Frank Billie, Henry Clay, Wilson Cypress, and Whitney Cypress (*Tampa Tribune* 1936).

In March 1937, the management of the Lake Wales attraction held a dubious "ceremony based on the spring festival of the tribes celebrated before the coming of the white man" (*Ft. Myers News Press* 1937b). During this festival, the Seminoles were extolled as "naturalists" in romanticized verse. W. Stanley Hanson was again the escort for seventy *i:laponathli:* (nearly one-fifth of the population) to the tower's annual event (ibid.; *Lake Wales News* 1937).

The marketing of the Florida Seminoles had come into its own. As the Seminole villages became some of Florida's most popular and longest running pre-Disney attractions, they gave the Seminoles a legacy that promoted alligator wrestling, a growing appreciation of arts and crafts, and significant support of their "unconquered" status.

CHAPTER 4

The Statistics of
an Exhibition Economy

Their own private folkways have a cash value that must be bewildering.

Reverend James L. Glenn (1928)

The reticent *i:laponathli:* continued to flock to the tourist attractions, while the attractions presented new challenges beyond those previously experienced. Men were not overtly ambitious in their own society, as it was not considered "normal" behavior, and persons who deviated from the norm would be chastised, even killed, if they persisted. However, at the tourist attractions, an enterprising man was rewarded and given the most important and well-paying role that an *i:laponathli:* could have in the business, that of headman. This position was based on intelligence and a good command of English, because the headman was understood to have the responsibility of the camp's affairs. He handled the grocery money and granted and dispensed salaries. He also located additional families to fill vacancies at the attraction for the new season (West 1981:205; Davis 1980).

However, the clan system was the key to his selection. In the *i:lapo-nathli:'* matrilineal society, all of the women and their children in a traditional camp were of the same clan. The only outsiders were the husbands who came to live in the matrilocal residence. In keeping with this prescribed system, the headman's selection would have met with his wife's approval, and her kin usually filled the seasonal positions in the tourist attraction camp. The elder woman was in charge of her camp wherever it was located and represented the head of her clan within the confines of her camp. According to Ethel Cutler Freeman, the elder woman determined when the camp would move, where it would relocate, and "how her charges will meet economic problems" (Freeman 1944:125). It was thus the *i:laponathli:* women who ultimately sanctioned their families' significant economic move to the tourist attractions (West 1983:13). As she was the actual head of the tourist attraction camp, she involved herself in other camp affairs as well, making many decisions that appeared to come from her husband. She was the silent partner, for women were not to speak to whites unless they were old acquaintances. *I:laponathli:* women transacted much of their business through their husbands or male relatives until the 1940s.

The attractions provided a constant seasonal income. Nash's statistics show "about $6 per week per family plus food," which appears to be fairly accurate (Nash 1931:39). Itemized expenditures at Musa Isle Seminole Village for the week of March 24–30, 1932, break down payroll and give a total grocery allowance per participant: "Cory Osceola, headman, $10.00; Josie Billie, $5.00; Mrs. Futch Cypress, $7.50; Mrs. Jimmie Billie, $2.50; William McKinley Osceola, $7.50; Tommie Billie, $3.00; groceries, $25.00." Changes in camp residence can be seen in the fluctuating payroll amounts, not itemized here, and the grocery allowance for two dates in April: "4/2/32, payroll, $33.00; groceries, $25.00; 4/9/32, payroll, $24.50; groceries, $20.00" (Dade County Chancery Records 1932).

Additional income at the tourist attractions was gleaned from tips for allowing photographs. Phil James of Coppinger's recalled that the *i:laponathli:* would turn their backs on a photographer unless they got a tip. They would accept pocket change but usually got a quarter (James 1981). Florence I. Randle, a Works Progress Administration photographer working in the 1930s, gave her subjects cloth, beads, and cigarettes for posing (West 1996: 32). At the Silver Springs Indian Village the *Ocala Star* reported on the *i:laponathli:* families who came to that attraction from the Big Cypress: "The Seminoles in the village . . . are by now accustomed to a lot of American visitors. Hundreds go through there every week since the village is one of the main attractions offered at the resort. When a visitor wants to snap a picture of the Indians, the guide tells the Seminole: 'Yas-sah-putz' [evidently a nonsensical term]. Immediately the Indian strikes a pose, which consists mainly of raising to his or her feet and standing like Indians always stand, motionless and staring into no where" (Martin 1937).

There were special economic advantages for the *i:laponathli:* employed at Coppinger's Indian Village. The Coppingers held accounts with several merchants who allowed the Indian women to make purchases for their sewing needs, a set amount per family. With this added income, the salary per family was lower than at Musa Isle. The Coppingers' attraction was popular, however, and it was not uncommon for them to turn away families for lack of space in the village. However, they always saw that these families had something to eat (James 1980).

Often families returning to the attractions from the Everglades and the Big Cypress brought relatives who had never been to a tourist attraction village before. It would be hard to imagine the consternation they must have felt. Phil James (1980) recalled from his experience with Coppinger's Indian Village that these new initiates were "kind of shy, but they got used to it after awhile." If they did not like living in the attraction, they left. Alan Davis (1980) recalled that sometimes families would come to Musa Isle "in rags and the children looked like they hadn't enough to eat, and in three to four months they all had new clothes and they [were] getting fat." The Coppingers tried to be selective in choosing the families for their village, not taking in anyone who drank excessively.

The government's special Seminole agent, Roy Nash, included statistics on the Seminoles' tourist attraction economy for 1930 (Nash 1931). His figures show only eighty people, 20 percent of the *i:laponathli:* population, in residence at tourist attractions for the 1930 season. His data apparently came from his cursory observations made while discussing the Seminoles' hunting statistics with Bert Lasher at Musa Isle, as he only estimated how many families could reside in the camp's seven *chickees* (native houses) at one time (pp. 37–39). He was apparently unaware of the turnover of itinerants, those families who brought crafts to sell and hides to the trading post and who came for the purpose of earning temporary exhibition income. The number of itinerants is the critical figure in determining the seasonal statistics of this far-reaching economy.

Statistics from Musa Isle foreman Alan W. Davis, who resided at the attraction from 1925 to 1932, provide more facts. The year 1930 was a significant one for observing statistics on the *i:laponathli:'* participation in the exhibition and tourist-related economy. An estimated four hundred *i:laponathli:* were officially enumerated by Nash that year (1931:23). Based on statistics, it appears that at least one-half of the *i:laponathli:* population resided at some time in a tourist attraction in 1930.

A family unit was estimated by Davis as five persons. Musa Isle had five families: twenty-five individuals; two additional campsites changed every three or four days, according to Davis (1980), or once weekly. In 1930, a season was an average of six months, January through June, or 182 days. Coppinger's had five *chickees*, or twenty-five individuals, and appeared to make room for visiting itinerants as well, although no estimates are available. Thirty to forty individuals were engaged in 1930 to live in a village opened by a realtor in St. Petersburg (Nash 1931:21; West 1981, 1986a).

It is again important to account for the critical multiple itinerant visits that Nash did not consider. At the same time the estimate should be conservative, assuming that duplication did occur. Therefore, the hypothesis might be presented that only ten itinerant families visited Musa Isle seasonally (five persons per family in Musa Isle's two vacant *chickees*), making two trips to the attraction during the 182-day season—an estimate of 110 persons, representing twenty-two different families. Add to that number the ninety permanent residents at the two Miami attractions and the one in St. Petersburg, and the total *i:laponathli:* population at the tourist attractions for the tourist season of 1930 is 50 percent.

This estimate is below the actual number of *i:laponathli:* who dealt with the attractions in 1930. The attractions had by then become a lucrative marketplace. In sixteen years of research I have never known of any *i:laponathli:* family that had not had some exhibition experience in past generations. In fact, I have interviewed only one person, Suzie Jim Billie (Panther) (1990), who said proudly that she never resided in a Miami attraction. However, she and her husband, Robert (Wind), were Big Cypress residents who, like other enterprising families, opened an attraction of their own on the Tamiami Trail in the 1930s, thus also becoming active participants in the tourist economy.

With the basic participant figures in place at the two Miami attractions, in the years 1931, 1933, and 1939 additional families attended large expos in the north. Silver Springs opened the large Indian Village in the mid-1930s. Additional *i:laponathli:* families like the Billies began building their own small tourist attractions along the Tamiami Trail in the late 1930s. Other families participated and supported the tourist economy by producing crafts for the tourist market, gathering baby alligators, and catching live alligators. My research is conclusive enough to state that all of the *i:laponathli:* population, and a significant portion of the *ci:saponathli:* population as well, were immersed in a tourist-based economy in the tourist seasons of the 1930s and 1940s.

By 1930, the non-Indians' commoditization of the *i:laponathli:* or the *i:laponathli:'* commoditization of themselves (depending on one's view of the situation) was at an all-time high. But the process did not have the negative effect on the *i:laponathli:* as it had had on some other native groups, such as the Hawaiians. The Hawaiians (and many other Pacific peoples) were reduced to the tourists' concepts of "hula dancers, ukuleles, and pineapples." As Keesing notes, "The commoditization of their cultures has left tens of thousands of Pacific Islanders as aliens in their own lands, reduced to tawdry commercialized representations of their ancestors, histories and cultures" (1989:32). The *i:laponathli:* were with few exceptions (such as the concept of "chiefs") treated as themselves, and the continuing commoditization of their sovereignty was a tribal plus, not a minus. W. Stanley Hanson of the Works Progress Administration's Writers' Program noted in 1930, "It is the consensus of authorities who have made a study of Indians of North America, that the Florida Seminoles are the most picturesque in the United States and this coupled with the fact that these Indians are the descendants of the only enemy that Uncle Sam has ever failed to conquer, makes them additionally attractive to visitors to the state" (WPA 1930).

CHAPTER 5

Traditions on Exhibition

She let down her hair.

Miami Herald, 1922c

It has long been a general assumption that *i:laponathli:* folkways were curtailed through their intense interaction with the tourist attractions, but my research has shown that their cultural life-style did not deviate greatly from that followed in their Everglades settlements. Changes in rudimentary subsistence tasks—tending gardens, processing cornmeal, and running hogs—were left behind, and clothing and crafts production emerged strongly in the daily routine at the tourist attractions. The men at both Musa Isle and Coppinger's were periodically engaged in hewing cypress dugout canoes for their personal use (Davis 1980; James 1980).

Because in this matrilineal society women and children of different clans never partook of food prepared over the same fire, having more than one clan in residence in the villages required some consideration—another reason for one clan to be dominant at an attraction. In the Musa Isle

Village two full-sized cooking *chickees* were utilized by the resident families and visitors of different clans (West 1981: 210), a situation not unlike that at the annual Green Corn Dance where each clan has its own camp and fire.

Although not always apparent to tourists, traditional customs were followed strictly. For instance, children at Musa Isle, Coppinger's, and Osceola's Indian Villages were sent to fetch water when a visitor arrived, a task that was one of their first social duties. A child slow to do so would be "scratched," the traditional punishment (Storm 1985). The number four, for the four directions (significant to many Native Americans), was observed as a time counter for songs, days of confinement, and many other customs. Women in the tourist attractions continued to isolate themselves during menses and childbirth and observed food restrictions and preparations at those times (Davis 1980; Holloway 1981; Lindsey 1981). Tourist attractions, then, would have afforded an opportunity to observe traditional customs at close hand.

Protecting the camp and its inhabitants from the detrimental side effects of death governed the ways of the living. Ghosts of recently departed family members might try to take the soul of a loved one with them, causing a living person to sicken and also die. Dropped food was (and is) never touched, as surely it was a ghost who had wanted it. Such strict customs were observed for all major phases of life and death to protect not just individuals but the entire camp (Sturtevant 1967: 132).

Because of these beliefs, important restrictions and precautions were observed. If a person died in a camp, the camp had to be abandoned because it became dangerous to live there. In the Everglades camps, the birthing *chickee* was placed outside the camp perimeters to assure that a mother's possible death in childbirth would not mean that the camp would have to be abandoned. Childbirths at the Miami attractions followed this same procedure. At Musa Isle, children were born in a four-acre undeveloped area to the west of the village site. A canvas tarpaulin was erected over four posts to provide shelter for the mother, who was customarily assisted by one or two women of her clan. Also in keeping with custom, the father could not see his wife or child for four days, at which time they could reenter the camp (MacCauley 1887:497; Davis 1980). Children at Coppinger's were born in a traditional thatched *chickee* located to one side of the camp area (Davis 1980; James 1980). Births in the city attractions further indicate that these locations were not considered an adverse environment by the *i:laponathli:*.

On February 17, 1928, there was a death at Musa Isle Village. Edna Johns Tommie, who had been married to Tony Tommie in the sellout event of the 1926 season, had succumbed to tuberculosis, which had been diagnosed several months after the marriage ceremony. It was reported that "After the Indians' treatment had failed, Tony Tommie appealed to his wife's friends for aid." She was hospitalized, had an operation, and improved. Physicians recommended a change of climate. Bert Lasher "received the aid of the Miami Chamber of Commerce and other civic institutions to send Edna John to the mountains in West Virginia" (*Miami Herald* 1928a). She and Tommie were finally persuaded to make the trip, but after the arrangements were made she refused to leave the village and her condition worsened. A small *chickee* had been built for her in the undeveloped area outside the perimeters of the Indian Village and away from curious tourists. This location of a *chickee* for a sick person was also in keeping with traditions, as noted by anthropologist Alanson Skinner: "When the Indians residing in a permanent village believe a man is dying, they will carry him outside the village to die in a lodge hastily erected for the purpose, and thus avoid the necessity of moving camp to escape misfortune" (1913:74).

Alan Davis (1980) recalled that as soon as Edna Johns Tommie died, "The men . . . went to their huts and grabbed their guns and started shooting in the air. . . . [Then the] medicine man had to come in and make medicine, boil roots and so forth and anyone that had to do with her or about her, had to take a bath in this medicine and drink it." Anthropologist William C. Sturtevant commented on the importance of such medicine to the well-being of the camp: "These medical procedures serve to prevent the soul from returning to camp from lonesomeness, and taking the soul of a relative with it when it leaves" (1967:342).

Also keeping with custom, Edna Johns Tommie was buried the day she died. Contrary to custom, however, she was not placed in the traditional aboveground coffin and laid to rest in a secluded hammock. She was interred at Miami's Woodlawn Park Cemetery with all of her personal effects (*Miami Herald* 1928a, b).

At the Musa Isle Seminole Village, the prescribed death rites continued in the undeveloped area of the property. The *Miami Herald* noted, "Some distance from the village the Indians conducted ceremonies throughout the day and into the night except for the brief interval of the burial. Tony Tommie and other relatives of Edna John will remain in mourning four days following Seminole custom. The leader plans to leave today for some point in the Everglades to mourn alone." "Probably the last act of Tony Tommie before his departure into the Everglades was to fire a gun four times, once south, once east, once west, and once north. This ceremony completed he tied the gun to a tree and left it" (1928a, b).

Sturtevant's informants discussed the subject of gunfire used ceremonially in conjunction with a death in a camp in a similar situation. Another informant said that the gunfire was "to scare away the soul or hurry it along its way to the west" (1967: 339)—a practice that continues today following the funerals of traditional believers and most Christians. The other members of the Musa Isle Seminole Village continued such preventive postmortem customs as pouring "water [medicine]" on their heads and bodies, which would offer them further protection from the soul of the deceased woman (*Miami Herald* 1928b).

Especially harmful was the ghost of a bad person or a person who had suffered a violent death. At Coppinger's Tropical Gardens, Jack Tiger Tail was shot and killed on March 8, 1922. Following the murder, which took place in the middle of the night, the inhabitants of Coppinger's Village showed their distress over this overpowering threat to their well-being. A reporter noted, "Not a word was spoken and the silent figures, from the oldest squaw to the youngest child, kept the silence for hours." Fires were kindled in the camp and were kept smoldering with green wood to scare away the ghost of Jack Tiger Tail (*Miami Herald* 1922c, d). His wife and children moved from their *chickee* to a more secluded one.

> In her new abode, at the rear of the square elevated floor, she partitioned off a small space, of about three by six feet, and placed about a substance similar to a mosquito bar. She removed from her neck the long strings of beads. . . . Her hair had been "done up" on the top of her head but now she arranged it so that it laid over her shoulders. She donned a dress of blue and black . . . and went into seclusion behind the screen, where she shall 'sleep' for the next four days, or as long as the fires smoulder in the camp. During the next four days, she will not leave her seclusion, will eat but very little and will converse with no one. At the end of the four day period Mrs. Tigertail will come from her place of hiding, and with her hair still streaming down her back, and without the beads, will resume the usual activities of the camp.
> . . . Other women in the camp also went into mourning by undoing their hair on top of their heads. They retained possession of the beads, however. (*Miami Herald* 1922c)

The sensationalism of the murder, coupled with Tiger Tail's extreme popularity in Miami and Hialeah, created a media blitz. The *Miami Herald* reported on March 9, "Every copy of last Thursday's *Herald* containing the picture of Jack Tiger Tail, that was possible to obtain, was sold to persons who wished to send it to friends. The *Herald* has obtained another fine photograph of the slain chieftain and will put it in Tuesday's issue. Orders should be telephoned today for copies in order that all may be served." The *Herald* also solicited funds to provide for Mrs. Tiger Tail and her children. By March 31, over $1,500.00 had been collected" (1922g).

The white community asked and received permission from his relatives for burial. Tiger Tail's body lay in state at the King Undertaking Parlor for three hours before the funeral. "Hundreds of men, women, and children looked upon the casket." To be interred with Tiger Tail were the customary male grave goods, his rifle and a box containing all of his possessions: cooking utensils, an old flashlight, pieces of leather, buckles, knives, mirrors, small pieces of iron, beads, and other miscellaneous items. There is no mention of these items being "broken," which is the usual procedure. Also puzzling is the type of leather included in the burial. Perhaps it was cowhide, as buckskin was not traditionally interred with the dead as it was feared that all of the deer would go with the dead person (*Miami Herald* 1922d; Sturtevant 1967:335–36, 339, 345).

Alligator wrestler Henry Coppinger, Jr., was a key mourner, walking in front of the hearse on the way to the Miami City Cemetery. Hundreds witnessed the burial. Tiger Tail's was the first death to occur in the immediate confines of a tourist attraction. The violence associated with it was a further stigma which could threaten the well-being of the village residents. The Coppinger family feared that the Indians might leave the attraction for good. Undoubtedly special rites and cleansing ceremonies were carried out to assure that the camp would be safe, such as washing in medicine for four months and burning bay leaves, and the *i:laponathli:* stayed, saying they were "satisfied" (*Miami Herald* 1922d, f).

Jack Tiger Tail's popularity continued after his death. The Indian Village at Coppinger's came to be called the Tigertail Indian Village, and as late as 1926 it was billed as the "home of the late Chief Tigertail" (*Happenings in Miami* 1926). His murder was initially attributed to a white man who appeared the perpetrator through circumstantial evidence, and public opinion and outrage came close to sentencing him. However, the murder was actually committed by an *i:laponi:* resident of the village as retribution for adultery committed by Tiger Tail. Tiger Tail's termination was apparently considered justifiable by the tribal council (West 1981: 211–212; McIver 1993).

Another incident involving customs related to death illustrates a situation unique to some families who resided in the city attractions (as well as some on the federal reservation). They became dependent on city burials, perhaps based on their experiences with Jack Tiger Tail and Edna

Johns Tommie. Acculturation may have been at work, but there is also the expediency of disposing of the deceased in a timely manner, an important traditional custom and consideration. Residing in the city meant a great deal of planning and physical effort to move the body miles away to a suitably isolated site for an aboveground burial. It also required spending far more time in close proximity with the deceased, which was not advantageous for the living. The government field nurse, Charlotte Conrad, reported in 1940 that parents living in a Miami attraction put their dying three-year-old daughter in their car and drove out of town to the Tamiami Trail, where the little girl expired. According to the nurse, the parents "would not take the body back to the Amusement Park Village where they were living. They wanted it buried at Dania, by the Government" (Freeman 1940). Doubtless in this case it was the attraction's owners who did not wish the expense of the burial, so they requested that the government pay for it.

I:laponathli: were also taken out of the state to northern exhibitions (see chapter 8), which created unusual circumstances when deaths occurred. At the State Fair of Texas in Dallas in October 1932, an older Indian, (Tom) Homespun Billie (Otter), became ill with "stomach trouble." He was hospitalized but died. This situation "threw the village into a frenzy of mourning. An all night ceremony was followed by burial rites at Oak Cliff Cemetery" (Wiley 1985:110). Alan Davis had telegraphed William McKinley Osceola, his *i:laponi:* contact in Florida, to ask if Homespun Billie's body should be shipped home. Osceola wired back, "Bury him in Dallas. Dead Indian no good!" (Davis 1980). It was fortunate that Billie did not die in the exhibition camp, but Frank Willie (Bird) was on this trip and his nephew, Larry Mike Osceola, noted in 1982 that "most Indians know how to make medicine to keep the spooks away. In all probability my Uncle Frank Willie . . . fixed the medicine." While camp members were observing the rites, Davis buried Homespun Billie at dawn in order to evade the reporters.

Another major tour featured fifty *i:laponathli:* (12 percent of the population) at the New York World's Fair in 1939. Unfortunately a tragedy occurred during that seven-month exhibition. Mrs. John Billie slipped and fell in the wash area of the attraction, hitting her head and dying instantly. Her body was removed by the state's medical examiner with the help of Alan Davis. The *i:laponathli:* found themselves in dire circumstances as there was apparently no one in attendance capable of making medicine. Davis called William McKinley Osceola in Miami; he contacted the medicine man, Josie Billie, who was flown directly to New York.

The members of the New York exhibition camp had not eaten for forty-eight hours when Billie arrived. He brought with him all the necessary herbal preparations for making medicine. It was night when he arrived, and fires had been lit around the camp to ward off the ghost. He worked all night on the medicine and in the morning lined up everyone to wash in it. "Men were taking their shirts off and poring that stuff all over them and drinking it," recalled Alan Davis (1981a), who was considered especially vulnerable as he had helped remove Mrs. Billie's body. He was passed a cup of the medicine. "I drank some of it and I liked to have gagged. It was just . . . like quinine!" (1980).

Ethel Cutler Freeman, who wintered with the *i:laponathli:* in Big Cypress for a number of years, visited the New York Village from her home in Morristown, New Jersey. She observed that the death of Mrs. John Billie had an impact on the *i:laponathli:* in Florida as well. Unlike the case of William McKinley Osceola's dictum for Homespun Billie, "Mrs. Billie's body was sent back to her people where it was received with unusual rituals and rites. Josie [Billie] ordered the people to eat king-fish, but as these were unobtainable, another kind of fish seemed to be satisfactory" (1947: 3, 8).

Another event that created a sensation in the *i:laponathli:* community unfolded in Miami's Seminole Indian Villages. An execution decreed by the *i:laponathli:* council was carried out at Musa Isle on February 24, 1938. The victim was Johnny Billie (Panther), thirty years old. Billie had been condemned to death at the 1937 Green Corn Dance for two unrelated murders he had committed while intoxicated. He managed to stay alive only by residing for some time under the protection of the Seminole agent at the Hollywood Reservation. But he left the reservation, went to Miami, and, following an argument, assaulted two women at Coppinger's Village (Jimmie O. Osceola 1996a). The elderly father of one of the women, John Osceola (Panther), met with a hastily convened group of council members who granted him permission to carry out the execution immediately.

The media was on the scene to observe and record the events that followed. A number of attraction employees and *i:laponathli:* observers were witnesses to various scenes of this drama. The infirm Osceola was driven by his son in a pickup truck from Coppinger's to Musa Isle, where Billie was staying. When they reached Musa Isle, the son called for Billie to come out of the village on the pretense of doing some mechanical work on his truck (C. Cypress 1991). While this ploy did get Billie out of the confines of the village, all witnesses agreed that he was well aware of his fate and "walked knowingly into the shotgun blast which killed him"

(Sturtevant 1967: 386). The trigger of the sixteen-gauge shotgun was pulled by John Osceola (*Miami News* 1938c).

Charles Hamilton, who ran the souvenir shop at Coppinger's, observed, "The Indians, solemnly paraded about the spot [where Johnny Billie had fallen] with smoking green branches of trees. This was to drive away the spirit of Johnny Billie." "Driving back to his hut, Chief Osceola, seated cross legged before his hut with his gun across his knees and a pipe in his mouth, informed his tribesmen what he had done. They filed by him to shake his hand and gave him money, which the chief deposited in a tin can on the ground beside him." "Before too long, he had received $25–$30." It was further related, "Under the Seminole custom, Chief Osceola must sit for three days after the killing [a total of four days]" (*Miami News* 1938a, b, e).

The police arrived at Coppinger's, and John Osceola was taken into custody. This treatment surprised him. He was later released in the custody of his lawyer, O. B. White. The night of March 3, before Osceola's hearing, Charles Hamilton said that Osceola was up all night making medicine. "This was a brew of certain green leaves, kept in motion while boiling by one of the Indians who blew down a piece of bamboo into the fluid. [This medicine was probably prepared by medicine man, Josie Billie, who happened to be in Miami at the time.] Next morning, all of the Indians washed in it." On March 4, the hearing took place before the justice of the peace and Josie Billie acted as interpreter. According to the *Miami News* (1938c, d), "Perhaps the strongest defense witnesses for Chief Osceola will be Johnny Billie's own kinsmen, who, it is said, will testify the death sentence was submitted by them and they had given their approval." After ten minutes deliberation, the coroner's jury held the shooting of Johnny Billie by John Osceola to be justified. At noon on March 5, John Osceola broke his two-day fast. The *i:laponathli:* families at Coppinger's and Musa Isle began a feast which lasted several days.

Yet not everyone was pleased with the course taken by *i:laponathli:* justice (and doubtless the way the Indians' actions were accepted by the non-Indian public). Seminole agent F. J. Scott felt that John Osceola should be punished. In correspondence with Miami chief of police H. Leslie Quigg prior to the inquest, Scott stated,

In any man's land a murder is a murder, and cannot be condoned when it is premeditated, cold blooded murder . . . and I know of no good reason why a law of the land should not prevail in this case. . . .
Insofar as tribal approval of such an offense is concerned, it can

readily be seen how such an offense could be condoned by the members of the Seminole tribe who might be sympathetic, but mere tribal approval of the offense should not operate to appease the white man's law.

When an Indian leaves a government reservation set aside for his exclusive use and makes his home in any civilized community he immediately becomes subject to all of the laws of that community regardless of what his tribal customs and practices might have been.
. . .

It is not understood how we can teach the Seminoles to respect and obey the laws if major crimes committed in those communities are to be overlooked on the theory that the crime was committed in accordance with an ancient tribal custom. (*Miami Herald* 1938a)

Agent Scott, of course, was not in a position to condone the breaking of laws of the United States or to appreciate that the *i:laponathli:* at that time had their own laws firmly in place which, since they were non-reservation Indians, had not been questioned in a U.S. court. No one had formally notified the councilmen that they were not to handle their own affairs or the general population of *i:laponathli:* that they were not to obey tribal edicts. Scott did not, however, quote the Seven Major Crimes Act passed by Congress in 1885 which "took away major criminal jurisdiction from Indian tribes" (Deloria and Lytle 1984:4). Perhaps he realized that the jurisdiction over these nonreservation Indians was in a gray area of the law.

Attorney O. B. White got Osceola acquitted. However, Louis Capron, who was knowledgeable of "Seminole" customs and a close acquaintance of both the *i:laponathli:* and the *ci:saponathli:*, has recorded that during Billie's previous *i:laponathli:* council trials he had been "turned over to the Tiger [Panther] Clan for disposal" (1953:197). Thus, White was astounded when at the next Green Corn Dance, Osceola was put on trial by his own people for murder! White confided to a writer twenty years later, "You see, he [Osceola] hadn't been appointed the official executioner [after all]. He'd broken the Seminole code and taken the law into his own hands. I defended him before the [*i:laponathli:*] council and the trial lasted seven days. They never told me the verdict. But the old man died within a short time. I don't know to this day whether his death was natural or a legal Indian execution" (Burman 1959:204).

The tourist attraction Seminole villages were truly an environment in which non-Indian documenters and the most traditional element of the *i:laponathli:* could have mingled. Customs, tribal history, and personal accounts never before or since observed or related could have been recorded, and this information could now serve as important tribal resource material. Collecting such field research information would have been virtually impossible anywhere but in the attraction villages. The tourist villages were perhaps the most different from the Everglades camps in this respect, as it appears that research could have been possible in the city camps under the right conditions. Further, the subjects would have been the finest, as the *i:laponathli:* residing in the attractions came from an intensely traditional upbringing, growing to adulthood with most of the postwar period customs in place. But, except for ethnomusicologist Frances Densmore's studies in the 1930s (published in 1956), the tourist attraction villages were shunned by fieldworkers who viewed them as "commercial" and not worth serious research. They believed the "Seminoles" who worked there were "not like those in the Everglade camps"—in other words, not traditional. In retrospect, a great opportunity was missed.

CHAPTER 6

Saurians and Seminoles

Now, see if you can wake this alligator up!

Announcer, Alligator Wrestling Show

"There's the man who invented it," said Howard Osceola (Bird) pointing to a photo of pioneer alligator wrestler Henry Coppinger, Jr., at a photo exhibition at Seminole Fair. "We picked it up. Everybody wanted to get on the gravy train" (Howard Osceola 1995).

The alligator and the Seminole came together as a major tourist attraction feature around 1919 when young *i:laponathli:* men began wrestling for tips at Musa Isle following Henry Coppinger's instantaneous success at the Tropical Garden's Alligator Farm. Musa Isle's wrestling shows, shown on Pathé Newsreels in the nation's movie theaters, so popularized alligator wrestling that it became an activity synonymous with the Florida Seminoles. From that time on, virtually every attraction or carnival show that hired a Seminole family included alligator wrestling demonstrations.

Today, tourists continue to be amazed at this hazardous occupation. A reporter noted in the *Miami Herald*, "*That* is the draw of alligator wrestling, the danger, the lurking possibility that the alligator, instead of just lying there, will do something about the man on his back" (Bartlett 1983). But the *i:laponathli:*' economic relationship with alligators went back much farther. The underbelly of the alligator was prized by the European leather industry in the late 1870s (Ober 1875:184), and by the next decade the trade was well established with "as many as 50,000 hides shipped annually from Florida" (Hanna and Hanna 1948:343).

Alligator eggs were also a commodity. In the 1890s, at Frank Stranahan's pioneer trading post on New River at Fort Lauderdale, the eggs were incubated in moist leaves and sold to early tourists for twenty-five cents to a dollar each (Craig and McJunkin 1971:48). By 1910, Stranahan was buying as many as 5,000 alligator eggs at one time from the Indians at a nickel each. When they hatched, he would sell them to businesses in Jacksonville, which in turn paid twelve and a half to sixteen and a half cents each (Kersey 1975:55).

The baby alligator market continued into the twentieth century, providing souvenirs for tourist attractions. From Musa Isle and Coppinger's they were shipped by mail in small cardboard boxes all over the United States. Henry Coppinger, Jr., was concerned about the care they would receive and included detailed instructions with his shipments (Coppinger 1975). As noted in chapter 4, supplying the baby alligator market for the tourist trade was an activity in which even the *ci:saponathli:* could participate, miles away from the major tourist center of Miami. Billy Stewart (Panther), who lived near Lake Okeechobee, was an important source. He sent Coppinger a telegram in May 1923 saying, "Have 85 baby alligators for sale can you come and get them?" (Stewart 1923). Sam Tommie (Panther), one of Annie Tommie's sons who as a boy may have sold baby alligators to Frank Stranahan, was also involved in gathering up alligator eggs near Lake Okeechobee, where he was residing in 1937. He had received an order for 500 baby gators for which he expected to receive fifteen to twenty cents each (*Florida Times Union* 1937).

Both *i:laponathli:* and *ci:saponathli:* hunters were involved in the alligator hide market. They had little competition from white hunters before World War I, although the decline of this lucrative market was in sight (Kersey 1975:129). During the depression, however, alligator hunting took an upswing as both white and Indian hunters sought to increase their income by selling hides. When Bert Lasher went bankrupt at Musa Isle in 1932, the village headman William McKinley Osceola and foreman Alan W. Davis went into the hide business by staking *i:laponathli:* hunters. They would drive the hunters through the seasonally dried Everglades to a hunting area, drop them off with sufficient supplies, and pick them up ten days later. The low areas surrounding hammocks were made into micro-cosmic environments by the saurians called "alligator holes," and there alligators were to be found. The holes were usually about two to three miles apart. According to Davis, "If you could get six alligator hides a day, that was a good day's work [at 50 cents a running foot]" (Davis 1980). The hunters would bring back their cache of salted, rolled hides and, after a week's rest, would be dropped off in the Everglades again. Special inves-tigator Roy Nash noted in his 1930 survey that alligator hides were the major product of Seminole hunters (1931:36).

Coppinger's also handled some Everglades products brought in by the *i:laponathli:*, but not on the scale of the Musa Isle Trading Post. Hides, pelts, live animals, and various sizes of alligators were purchased to supplement the attraction's zoo, taxidermy shop, and alligator farm. Zoos were a common feature at most Seminole village tourist attractions, and most displayed native animals (see chapter 10).

The Seminole village attractions also did a brisk wholesale business in other alligator-related goods around the state and country. Small alliga-tors called "hornbacks" were mounted and made into souvenir curios such as lamp bases. They were often posed holding umbrellas or lightbulbs in their mouths. But the importation of the South American cayman cur-tailed this lucrative economy for the Florida Seminoles (Kersey 1975: 129).

While the veteran alligator wrestlers have credited Henry Coppinger with promoting the sport, they emphatically stress the fact that *i:lapo-nathli:* men were adroit in their handling of alligators in the wilds long before Coppinger began his tourist shows. Their skills also made them responsible for catching most of the alligators for the wrestling shows and alligator farms.

In the wild, when alligators are not swimming or basking in the sun, they live in a den under the bank of the alligator hole. Alan Davis de-scribed how they caught live alligators: "The Indian got in the water and as the gator come out of the cave . . . right between their legs. . . . they would grab the gator by the mouth and wrap the inside of their knees around the legs of the alligator." The gator would then begin spinning, but in the end it was captured. A safer method was to noose the alligator with a rope. "We'd put a noose over their cave and when [the gator would] come through, he'd go to rolling and we'd have . . . probably a hundred foot of rope. First thing you know, he's completely tied up. All we had to do was drag him out, tie his mouth up and tie his legs up over his back"

(Davis 1980). According to Coppinger's friend and employee Phil James, the *i:laponathli:* were paid according to the weight of their prize. The most he recalled paying for a large gator was twenty-six dollars (James 1980).

These shows were a big draw and brought the tourists into the Seminole villages. Before the young *i:laponathli:* men could enter this lucrative profession, however, they were supposed to ask permission of an old Snake Clan Woman (related to the extinct Alligator Clan), as it was not normal behavior for the *i:laponathli:* to tease or taunt an animal (Billie 1991). However, Betty Mae Tiger Jumper, a Snake Clan member who was raised a Christian, recalled, "We used to drag them out and have a game to see who could put one to sleep first" (Betty Mae Jumper 1994:27).

As commercial alligator wrestling was a new phenomenon, the elders doubtless shook their heads at the young wrestlers who were caught up in the economic frenzy of its popularity, wrestling for tourists' tips. Veteran alligator wrestler Alan Jumper (Panther) (1980) said that the money an alligator wrestler could make overcame the customs that questioned this activity. A contemporary wrestler, William (Chubby) Osceola, grandson of William McKinley Osceola, told a crowd, "The Indian does not believe in abusing or teasing the animal. We respect the gator. The gator and the Indian go together as part of nature. That is what I have been told by my grandfather. If others don't respect the animal, that is their problem" (Gallagher 1982).

Alligator wrestling has been described as "a type of theatrical performance" (Sturtevant 1971:121), but catching alligators, even being in the pen with them, is risky. In 1928, Josie Jumper (Bear) was bitten severely on the arm by a newly penned gator at Coppinger's "just caught west of Palm Beach" and measuring "over ten feet." "Close call," wrote an associate of the Coppinger family (anonymous ca. 1928). For a good wrestling show there is often a large margin of risk, and casualties were and are not uncommon.

A wrestling incident at the New York World's Fair in 1939 caused some excitement. Headlines read: "Two Bullets to the Brain." "The Indian as is his custom dived into a pool with 12 alligators. He grappled with 'Big Cypress' as a small group of spectators looked on. Suddenly, the saurian seized the Indian by the arm and began to twist. His jaws could not be pried open. Alan Davis, superintendent of the Seminole Indian Village, drew a .38-caliber automatic. Spectators were herded to one side. Davis held the barrel near the alligator's eye and fired twice. The department of sanitation was called to come and remove a dead alligator, 8 1/2 feet long and considerably in the way" (International News Service 1939).

Among the feats of showmanship that continue to be crowd pleasers today, the alligator wrestler places his head in the alligator's open jaws. Frank Jimmie (Wild Cat) performed this act around 1931 at an event in Palm Beach. It was a fad in those days for young Seminole men to wear their hair slicked straight back from their foreheads. Jimmie's hair fell forward, touching the alligator's sensitive palate. The jaws snapped shut. The gator was shot, but even then a crowbar had to be used to free Jimmie's head. While he did recover, Jimmie's ear and the side of his head were visibly damaged and crushed (Carter 1981). In 1935, the *i:laponi:* wrestler Riley Robenson of Osceola's Gardens Indian Village tried this stunt unsuccessfully and had to be hospitalized (*Miami Beach Tribune* 1935). In 1956, a writer who was interviewing Hollywood Reservation wrestler George Storm (Panther) noted scars on Storm's head from a similar accident (Burman 1956:151). Veteran wrestler Bobby Henry (Otter) has not forgotten the day his father, Jimmy Henry (Wild Cat), taught him that maneuver. As Bobby timidly placed his head between the gator's jaws, his father said, "Not like that. Like this!" He reached over and pushed the boy's head in farther (Henry 1995).

One six-year-old boy, identified only as Little Osceola, climbed over the fence at Osceola's Village and tried to wrestle a four-foot alligator for some visiting schoolchildren. His screams alerted his parents. He had been bitten on the leg. "Having seen his father entertain visitors to the park many times, Little Osceola told police he had thought it was easy" (*Miami Daily News* 1935).

"Tore up thumbs. Mangled toes. What drives a man to get in a scrap with a gator?" wrote a reporter in 1993 (Franke 1993). The top alligator wrestlers at Musa Isle in the 1920s were Josie Jumper, Henry "Cowboy" Billie, Chestnut Billie, and Frank Jimmie. In the 1930s and 1940s at Musa Isle they were Henry Sam Willie (né Henry Nelson), L. Mike Osceola, Bobby Tiger, Johnny Tigertail, and Johnny Jim. At Osceola's Indian Village there was Bill Osceola; at the *Jungle Queen* Indian Village, Ft. Lauderdale, Jack Motlow; and at Tropical Paradise, Joe Jimmie (Davis 1980; Carter 1981; L. Mike Osceola 1982; Dan Osceola 1995). In the 1950s and 1960s Moses Jumper performed at the *Jungle Queen* Indian Village. When he could not perform, his wife, Betty Mae Jumper, a future Seminole tribal chairwoman, filled in as the only known Seminole woman alligator wrestler (Starts 1986; Jumper 1994:16). Other wrestlers from this period were Robert Osceola and Bobby Osceola (Silver Springs Seminole Village); Jackie Willie (Okalee Indian Village); Dan Osceola (Okalee and *Jungle Queen* Indian Village); Robert Bert (Pippin and *Jungle Queen* Indian Villages); George Billie (Aqua Glades Indian Village); Alan Jumper,

Henry Bert, "Wild Bill" Osceola, George Storm, Stanlo Johns (a *ci:saponi:*), and Teddy Nelson. In the 1970s and 1980s, Paul Bowers, Barney Tommie, Mike Clay, William "Bo" Jim, and Seminole tribal chairman James E. Billie performed, in the 1990s tribal chairman James E. Billie, Richard Bowers, Thomas Storm, Elvis "Tippy" Cypress, William "Chubby" Osceola, Stephen Billie, Kenny Cypress, and Paul Simmons.

The wrestlers had mentors in the business. Bobby Henry, whose career spanned forty-eight years, said that his mentor was "Cowboy" Billie (Big Towns). The performance he liked best was when Cowboy rolled over and over with his legs wrapped around the alligator until he had the alligator on its back, resting on his own chest. The gator would then pass out and the crowd would applaud (Henry 1995). James E. Billie wanted to be "just like Bobby Tiger [Bird]" (Billie 1995). Alligator wrestling led to the creation of a modified popular garment. James Billie attributes the origins of the short-sleeved patchwork alligator wrestling shirt to Bobby Tiger's long career, yet it was Billie's greater visibility that popularized this garment, and most consider it the "James Billie" shirt.

At the climax of an alligator wrestling performance, the wrestler would flop the alligator on its back and stroke it to sleep. An announcer at Musa Isle in the 1930s would say to the audience at this point, "The alligator wrestler doesn't receive any pay from the Village for putting on this exhibition. The only money he gets is what you throw into the pool. . . . Now see if you can wake this alligator up!" (Davis 1980). Announcers continued this spiel at Musa Isle well into the 1940s (and even today) (Freeman 1941a:6). If a wrestler gave a good show to an enthusiastic audience, he might get a week's salary in a day.

Ethel Cutler Freeman thought initially that the tourist attractions were degrading to the *i:laponathli:*. She further targeted alligator wrestling because she was specifically put off by the way alligator wrestlers received their tips. The idea of someone "throwing money" was, in light of her own social upbringing, distasteful. She was therefore astonished when she questioned one of the non-Indian alligator wrestlers, Tommy Carter, about his feelings on the subject: "[He] wrestles with alligators at Musa Isle and gets money thrown to him. They do not feel that this is belittling them" (1941b).

A writer for *Reader's Digest* described another method of "waking the alligator up" as performed by Josie Jumper at a tourist attraction on the banks of New River in Fort Lauderdale in 1956: "For some time Josie Jumper allowed the beast to lie inert, then leaned close to its head and began to grunt as I have heard an alligator grunt in the marshes. The monster suddenly came to life, and the beaming Josie passed the hat for the usual collection" (Burman 1959:151). "Passing the hat" or the basket has become the more accepted form of receiving tips.

A number of non-Indian alligator wrestlers performed professionally. At Musa Isle, foreman Alan Davis filled in for *i:laponathli:* wrestlers in the years 1922 to 1932. Tex Farless and Phil Wofford's duties at Musa Isle and at the 1939 New York World's Fair included wrestling when they were needed. Tommy Carter began wrestling at Musa Isle during a slow summer in 1932 when Musa Isle's key performer "Cowboy" Billie was away, and he remained at the attraction until 1942. Just before he left, he taught young Bobby Tiger the fine points of wrestling (Carter 1981). Bill McClellan starred at the Hollywood Chimpanzee Farm with Guy LaBree as his stand-in. Tommy Taylor, head of the Seminole Tribe's Kissimmee Billie Swamp Safari, is a veteran wrestler. Paul "Swamp Owl" Morrison wrestled at Swamp Safari, which Mike "Skeet" Johns performed at Native Village in Hollywood.

Alligator wrestling was indeed a lucrative and legitimate occupation. Jackie Willie wrestled alligators in the Fort Lauderdale area while living in his *chickee* on the Dania Reservation. On November 3, 1956, he was affluent enough to sign notes with the Friends of the Seminole organization for a loan to begin construction of his family's interest-free, two bedroom home—only the fourth concrete block house built on the Dania Reservation to that date (West 1995a). In 1961 the *Seminole Indian News* noted that "Bobby Tiger and his family returned to Dania from Michigan, where he had spent the summer wrestling alligators at an attraction. They have moved into their $8,000 home on the Dania Reservation." During the same period, the family of alligator wrestler Robert Bert spent their seasons in the Wisconsin Dells (Mitchell 1998).

Jackie Willie was the star wrestler at the newly opened, federally funded Seminole Okalee Indian Village on the Hollywood Reservation in 1960. During Seminole Fair, held annually at the village, Richard Bowers (Panther) and Thomas Storm (Otter) have been the most recent "deep water" alligator wrestlers. Storm continues to perform. The alligator is located and grabbed in waist-deep water, a dangerous situation with an unpredictable gator, then dragged out onto the sand and wrestled. Wrestlers can earn $2,000 or more for a thirty-minute show. Bowers, now retired, said, "The alligator has escorted me all the way across the country and back again." He recalled that for years, the Speckled Perch "Chalo Nikta" festival at Moore Haven, Florida, hosted an alligator wrestling contest as part of their annual festivities. As many as ten wrestlers competed for the prize of five hundred dollars (Bowers 1993).

Many economic choices for young *i:laponathli:* men are more lucrative today than wrestling alligators, but there is something special about alligator wrestling, perhaps best summed up as skill, acclaim, and money. The crowds of tourists and festival goers continue to be spellbound—they gasp and cheer. While some cautious festival organizers around the state shy from including alligator wrestling for fear of retaliation from animal rights activists, there are still plenty of occasions, especially during festivals on the reservations, to witness this *i:laponathli:* sport. On birth certificates ("occupation of father") and death certificates ("occupation of deceased"), the occupation of alligator wrestler is a folkway which is a legitimate profession handed down from generation to generation with a great deal of pride.

CHAPTER 7

Commercial Wares

Seminole arts and crafts are Seminole life.

Alice L. Marriott, specialist in Indian arts and crafts, Indian Arts and Crafts Board, 1943

A long-lasting cultural and economic indication of the *i:laponathli:'* involvement in the tourist attractions was the commercialization of crafts. It led in turn to the further development of patchwork, their own distinctive form of artistic expression.

Prior to the tourist attraction economy, most energy was expended to achieve basic subsistence. Agent Lucien A. Spencer documented it in the racist overtones of his day: "The cause for the lack of progress among these Indians is and has been, a lack of a dependable source for subsistence. Their problem of securing food and clothing has heretofore taken all their time and left them no opportunity for mental development" (U.S. Department of the Interior 1918:6).

Indeed, one of the major time-consuming tasks was the women's preparation of the staple *coonti*. This product was made from the root of the native cycad, *coonti (Zamia floridiana)*, which was dug from the rocky coastal pinelands at the expenditure of considerable energy and entailing days of preparation. Eventually, a fine, white powdered starch was produced, one prized by the non-Indian community as well.

There were also hides to tan for trade, a varied assortment of edible plants and berries to be gathered in the wild, and droves of hogs (a woman's primary property) to tend. Although much work was shared between the sexes, these particular tasks were firmly in the women's domain. The all-important task of gardening was a responsibility shared by the entire extended family (West 1983).

Once the results of the drainage programs and a failing hide market forced the *i:laponathli:* into trying the new economic venue of the tourist attractions of Miami, the women began to enjoy the freedom from their daily responsibilities for subsistence. At the attractions where they became the commodity, the women could spend more time engaged in sewing clothing and making craft items (West 1981:208). The tangible encouragements provided by the attractions—sewing machines and fabric, for instance—cannot be overlooked as important incentives to motivate further the women's newly found leisure time and to aid them in expanding their creative potential (Coppinger 1975).

However, one early commercial venture created a cultural conflict. A craftsman was asked to make representative images for the commercial market, a family of wooden dolls commissioned for a Doll Land Convention in New York around 1900. According to one source, the craftsman who carved the dolls was afraid that his family would "get sick" because he had made representational images (Kersey 1975:114). Indeed, carved images were used by *i:laponathli:* sorcerers in making bad medicine (Sturtevant 1967:394).

Two different styles of wooden dolls gradually appeared on the market. One was made entirely of wood, carved and painted by the men. The other was carved by men and dressed in cotton clothes by the women, as were the ones for the New York show (West 1984:64).

Around 1918, the popular palmetto fiber dolls began to be offered at the tourist attractions. These mass-produced dolls are the type that continues to be produced today. The men carved toy cypress canoes. Both crafts were marketed out of the makers' *chickees* (James 1980). There were no organized outlets for Seminole crafts other than the city Seminole attractions and the *i:laponathli:'* Tamiami Trail villages that had opened by the mid-1930s. In the 1930s, women from the Everglades and even from the federal reservation at Dania made the long trip to Miami to sell these dolls in the attractions' gift shops (West 1981:209). The 1932 *Annual Report* from the Seminole Agency acknowledged an interest in Seminole arts and crafts, noting that the few villages on the Tamiami Trail "have very, very few items to offer the public. A crafts teacher could aid greatly in developing this opportunity. In fact many Indians from the northern and western United States come to the Miami area during the Winter season to capitalize on the tourist market. The local Indians should have the first right to this economic possibility" (U.S. Department of the Interior 1932:10).

In 1934, the enterprising *ci:saponathli:* women at Dania Reservation under matriarch Annie Tommie got their men to make them a small craft booth at the entrance gate to the reservation facing State Road 441. Ivy Stranahan noted that Seminole dolls were so popular at the booth that demand was often far greater than supply (Warren 1934:27; West 1986c). *Ci:saponathli:* women Rosalie Huff (Panther), Annie Tommie (Panther), and *i:laponathli:* Ada Tiger (Snake) were the "first people who started making the palmetto dolls" at Dania Reservation (Jumper 1988:1).

In 1941, doll sales were brisk near Ocala at the Silver Springs Village populated by *i:laponathli:* from the Big Cypress. Ethel Cutler Freeman visited and wrote, "They were making dolls of palmetto fiber to sell. Every one was making these. They had huge bundles of them, bigger than pillow cases full. I don't see how they will ever sell them all, the market will be glutted" (Freeman 1941a). But this attraction was receiving "upwards of 500,000 persons annually" in 1935 (*Tampa Tribune* 1935). It is actually doubtful that the women could keep up with such a souvenir-oriented market.

By the 1890s a growing number of *i:laponathli:* women owned sewing machines. From the accounts left by trading post operators, it can be seen that it was often the men who first learned how to operate these labor-saving devices, then communicated the operating instructions to their more reticent wives (Kersey 1975:138). The hand-cranked machine was the most popular model for use by the highly mobile *i:laponathli:* women. It could be packed with ease into a canoe, set up on a distant *chickee* platform, or used in temporary camps all across the Everglades. An excellent example of the versatility of the hand-cranked machine was witnessed by a Miami schoolgirl around 1915. She recalled walking through a tree hammock on her way home from school and seeing an *i:laponi:* woman sewing with her machine propped up on a fallen tree (Redman 1981).

The sewing machine meant that the Florida Seminoles' hand-sewn cotton clothing—which appeared little changed from the early nineteenth century—could be sewn more quickly by machine. In time the widespread use of the machine and the populating of south Florida by settlers caused clothing styles to change. Clothing was enhanced by the addition of the famous machine-sewn patchwork inserts, which would become the Florida Seminoles' distinctive art form (Blackard 1990: 44–45).

I:laponathli: artists excelled at patchwork, and as a result of their time spent "on exhibition" in the tourist attractions their art flowered. The attractions promoted the continued and enhanced wearing of patchwork clothing. The men, for instance, were on the verge of discarding native clothing. They had quit wearing their long patchwork belted shirts by the 1930s because the shirts could not easily be tucked into trousers, which by then all the men wore on the city streets. The women then began making "transitional" belted shirts with no bulky ornamentation beneath the belt line. By the end of the 1930s, the belted shirt simply terminated at the waistband, becoming the now famous Seminole patchwork jacket.

Ethnomusicologist Frances Densmore described the process of making patchwork in the 1930s:

> The cotton cloth used in making patchwork banding is fine, firm in texture, and preferably plain in color. The cloth is torn in strips and cut into blocks of the desired size and shape. For this purpose the women use very fine, sharp scissors with long, slender blades. The blocks are placed in little piles, each size by itself, ready for use. Thus a woman was seen with several piles of small squares and triangles near her left hand, on the edge of her sewing machine, where she could put them under the needle in the desired order, without basting. The women work at this task for many hours at a time, often with a phonograph playing as they work. The banding is made in long strips which are folded away, ready to be inserted in skirts and blouses, or in dresses [belted shirts] for little children or old men. The material and the finished banding are kept scrupulously clean, and the women are always neatly dressed when at work, with everything orderly around them. (Densmore 1956)

There was not a great demand for Indian clothing during the early years at the Miami Seminole Village tourist attractions, but garments could be ordered. Formal craft shops had opened at Coppinger's and Musa Isle by 1922 (West 1981:208).

Inventory records are a rarity, but as Lasher went bankrupt both Musa Isle and Osceola's Indian Village came under receivership. His misfortunes have thus provided a good record— the itemized receivers' inventories from 1932 to 1934. They show "[Toy] Indian canoes, bows and arrows, costumes, fiber Indian dolls, wooden Indian dolls, beaded bracelets, beaded rings, tom toms, and wooden spoons." With the exception of the wooden dolls, these items are still sold today. The receiver for Musa Isle noted that "the 'Indian merchandise' item is when we buy from the Indians such as dolls, dresses and men's shirts which they make and are very good sellers; we pay them in cash as they cannot read or write" (Dade County Chancery Records 1932).

Cory Osceola (Big Towns) was headman of the Musa Isle village from the late 1920s to 1932. Osceola, who had become literate as a result of his tourist attraction experience, managed the large-volume Musa Isle Trading Post concession at this major attraction (Holloway 1981). In that position, he assumed a greater business responsibility than had any *i:laponi:* since the late Willie Willie (West 1987b). Meanwhile, Osceola and his brother William McKinley were active buyers of *i:laponathli:* crafts along the Tamiami Trail. Shrewd businessmen, it appears that they instituted the first formal quality-control measures on crafts (Johns and Cypress 1996).

A pictorial brochure from Musa Isle about 1929 shows the variety of crafts and souvenir novelties made by the *i:laponathli:* for sale. The brochure notes, "We are selling many interesting and valuable articles, souvenirs and costumes that we carry in stock at all times. Your orders will always have our prompt and careful attention and we guarantee safe delivery" (Musa Isle ca. 1929). "Dolls-Indian" were fifty cents to three dollars. Most items were *i:laponathli:*-made, although the "rugs, zarapes Tekeelah Wall Placques, and Indian pottery" were not. The native Seminole clothing, listed under "Dresses-Indian," ranged between three and ten dollars. Some early examples of skirts documented for commercial sales show that either because non-Indians preferred a less full skirt or because the *i:laponathli:* women were making them for commercial consumption and not for themselves, less yardage was used.

In 1933, a semiretired sixty-year-old Episcopalian deaconess, Harriet M. Bedell, arrived in southern Florida. When she was shunned by *i:laponathli:* while visiting a Miami attraction, she assumed that their attitude was caused by their "demeaning" dependence on the tourist economy. She vowed to wean them away from the atmosphere of commercialism by establishing a crafts cooperative. This she did, at Glade Cross Mission located in the tiny town of Everglade City in southwest Florida, south of the Tamiami Trail. The crafts program she instituted benefitted the Trail and Big Cypress families (West 1984).

In the 1930s, as Bedell's crafts cooperative gathered momentum, she promoted and suggested a number of items to her workers. Some of her suggestions caught on and were sold miles away in the Miami attractions: waste, work, market, and picnic baskets made out of traditional palmetto stem splints; grass pin cushions; patchwork and basket purses; patchwork pillow covers and lounge covers; and wooden plaques, bookends, buttons, plates, and bowls (Bedell 1935, 1941).

A series of patchwork designs from the 1920s through the 1950s were "named" by Bedell. She eventually singled out these designs as the only ones she would accept at the mission, creating an anomalous style within the mainstream development of patchwork art. Yet she was adamantly opposed to the introduction of pan-Indian artistic elements, introduced to the *i:laponathli:* by whites and Native Americans from other areas of the country who frequented the Miami attractions. She mentioned these intrusive elements in her mission mailings, noting that she encouraged the Seminoles to "develop an art of their own, not copying that of western Indians," but in the Miami attractions her dictum was not followed (West 1984:56, 63).

"Blue Bird," John Carillo, an Isleta Indian from New Mexico, came to Musa Isle in the 1930s. While there, he introduced oil painting and instructed the Florida natives in painting drums with southwestern motifs and silhouettes of Plains Indians in war bonnets (Carter 1981). In no time, these motifs appeared on toy Seminole canoes and other wooden items, where they can be found even today.

Musa Isle foreman Alan Davis purchased green calfskins and cured them into rawhide for the first drums made at Musa Isle. Drums became a popular item for sale. The "Tiger boys," specifically Buffalo Tiger (Bird), were the artists mainly involved in this project. Other exotic crafts were introduced by manager Nellie (Mrs. John A.) Campbell when she took over the attraction in 1932. She introduced "peace pipes" cut from the stands of giant bamboo that grew on the property. She also created an interest in continuing loom beadwork, an art that was dying out among native craftswomen who had produced ceremonial belts for the men. The women and girls began to use beads ordered by Campbell to produce bracelets, necklaces, rings, and belts to be worn with trousers, all for the commercial market. Seminole geometric designs and pan-Indian motifs were used and were popular with the tourists (West 1981:208).

Sonny Coppinger, Henry's youngest brother, recalled that it was around 1928 when the *i:laponathli:* men began to carve totem poles for Coppinger's Pirates Cove Seminole Village. The poles of native cypress wood were carved by Indian men, but it was the non-Indian employees who painted them (Downs 1981:227). Around 1938, Musa Isle commissioned Frank Willie and other craftsmen to make a number of poles for the Seminole Village facade. Tommie Carter (1981) recalled that Buffalo Tiger painted the poles, which were set in cement along the top of the rock wall forming the entrance to the attraction. The men also carved miniature totem poles to sell as souvenirs (West 1982:16).

Since the late 1920s, the multicolored poles have been erected throughout Florida at tourist attractions where Seminoles are employed. They can be seen at Indian-operated businesses and in front of tribal departments at the Hollywood, Big Cypress, and Tampa reservations and along the Tamiami Trail. The Seminole totem poles alert the tourist to the presence of a Seminole or Miccosukee Indian craft shop (West 1986b). Ethel Cutler Freeman (1941a) described the addition of ornamental totem poles to the Silver Springs Seminole Village attraction: "A large fence surrounds the village and topping this every 25 feet or so are incongruous brightly colored totem poles. I suppose to the casual tourist this is an added native touch and the management considers it decorative. Some of the Sem[inoles] now make models of totem poles because they can sell them to the visitors and the other junk, the tom toms, and the cheap bamboo rattles and the manufactured moccasins that the white owners of these Exhibitions tell the tourists ar[e] typical of the Seminoles is a crime. They tried to stuff me full of it and when I said that these were not the rattles that they used, they insisted that they were old time things. They had to save 'face'."

The management seemed to believe that the more elements from different tribal styles, the more willing tourists would be to pay their entry fee and visit the gift shop. Strengthening the selling power of Seminole crafts, the first craft program for reservation Seminoles began in 1940. With aid from the fledgling Indian Arts and Crafts Board in Washington, Edith M. Boehmer organized the Seminole Craft Guild on the *ci:saponathli:'* newly established Brighton Reservation northeast of Lake Okeechobee. The board had been created under Indian Commissioner John Collier's reorganization programs.

In 1952, anthropologist William C. Sturtevant took a special interest in *i:laponathli:* commercial crafts. He purchased examples for the Smithsonian's collections and noted, "The demand for these items is greater than can be met by the Seminoles, and economic returns from the work are relatively good. An approximate calculation at 1952 prices shows that a woman earns eighty or ninety cents an hour profit in this work, and families operating their own stores along the Tamiami Trail get greater returns by eliminating the middlemen and by themselves acting as middlemen for other Seminole producers" (1967:75).

The art of patchwork is most important to the *i:laponathli:* as it has given them not only their major art form but a blazon of tribal identity. In the past, tribal members on visits to other states or attending meetings in the nation's capital could guarantee that their tribal heritage would be duly noted. While some matrons continue to wear patchwork skirts daily, middle-aged men frequently wear jackets, vests, or baseball caps. Almost everyone has some patchwork garment to wear on special occasions to reinforce his or her identity. Alice Marriott, a specialist with the Indian Arts and Crafts Board, aptly noted on a visit to the Seminoles in the 1930s, "Seminole arts and crafts are Seminole life" (1943:50).

CHAPTER 8

Expositions, Fairs, and Failures

The Indians Are Coming!
Wildwood (N.J.) *Leader*, 1932

It took more than expensive electric signs to lure investors to South Florida during the early years of the 1920s. Major real estate promotions selling Florida land canvassed the Northeast and Midwest. These promotions succeeded, and the *i:laponathli:* inadvertently were caught up in the ensuing frenzy, ironically aiding in the promotional sale of the very land that their fathers and grandfathers fought so hard to retain during the Seminole wars. Shows with *i:laponathli:* "on exhibition" opened as far west as Texas, as far north as Canada.

In the late nineteenth century the Office of Indian Affairs had instituted regulations for promoters engaging reservation Indians for exhibition purposes. These regulations were strictly enforced by the depart-

ment, and the few applications granted had to post a $10,000 bond. Buf-
falo Bill Cody's famous Wild West show presented one of the applications
that was granted in 1896. Federal regulations on the exhibition of Native
Americans at that time read, "Whenever engagements with Indians for
exhibition purposes are made, their employers are required to enter into
written contracts with the individual Indians obligating themselves to pay
such Indians fair stipulated salaries for their services; to supply them with
proper food and clothing; to meet their traveling and needful incidental
expenses, including medical attendance etc. from the date of leaving their
homes until they return thither; to protect them from immoral influences
and surroundings; to employ a white man of good character to look after
their welfare, and to return them without cost to themselves and their
reservation within a certain specified time. They have also been required
to execute bond for the faithful fulfillment of such contracts" (U.S. Department of the Interior 1896:54).

The government felt that the exhibition economy which encouraged
nativism was not conducive to the assimilation of Native Americans into
mainstream society. The 1917 report from the Interior Department head
included an "exhibition" section: "Very few instances where the employment of Indians for exhibition purposes was desired came before me during the past year. In every case such employment was discouraged, and
only those were allowed to go who were not needed at home for farming
and other industrial pursuits on the ground that participation in such
exhibitions is not conducive to the formation of habits of industry and
thrift which I am endeavoring to inculcate among the Indians" (U.S.
Department of the Interior 1917:41).

Such regulations did not apply to the Florida Seminoles, for they were
not under government control. That is why, at the peak of their exhibition
involvement in the 1930s, there are no formal records of their move-
ments. However, the 1917 report did set the tone by which future government investigators and special commissioners to the "Florida Seminoles"
would judge the *i:laponathli:*.

Frank Stranahan, a leading Fort Lauderdale businessman by 1900,
planned to attend the Gala Week Fair in Jacksonville that year. He corresponded with the Florida East Coast Railroad to request free passage for
"a number of the Indian boys [who] have expressed a desire to go with me"
(Stranahan 1900). But the railroad did not see why the company should
"move Indians any cheaper than white men" (Parrott 1900), and the fair's
insurance company recalled that at a previous fair some of the *i:laponathli:*
participants had gotten intoxicated and "simply tore things up" (Bahl
1900), so Stranahan's request was denied.

The *i:laponathli:'* enthusiasm for such events appears to have been strong. Photos from the Seminole/Miccosukee Photographic Archive document attendance at fairs in southern Florida. Little Billie (Wind), who, with Little Tommie, had accompanied cattle baron Francis A. Hendry to the Florida State Fair in Jacksonville as a young man in 1884, took his own family to a Fort Myers fair early in the twentieth century. A photograph shows him posing with a complementary yardstick from the Seminole Lumber Company. In Miami, a group of *i:laponathli:* was photographed at a fair commemorating the fifteenth anniversary of the city of Miami in 1911 (Bratley 1911). Another photo shows *ci:saponi:* Billy Bowlegs III (Little Black Snake) wearing a ribbon from a fair with the message "Come and Get Me Girls and Candy!" (Seminole/Miccosukee Photographic Archive ca. 1900).

However, formally engaging a group of Florida Indians to participate in such events was not always easy. Promoter Edward Sadlow of Jacksonville took Byrd Frazier, a resident of Fort Myers who was close to the *i:laponathli:*, to help persuade some young men to attend the 1889 Sub Tropical Exhibition in Jacksonville. However, elders told the young men who showed interest in going that "if they went they should never come back to the tribe" and the promoter came home empty-handed (*Madison Recorder* 1889). In another situation an "old chief" did not want the younger men to attend a fair because "'Big sleep come pretty quick if go . . . Billy Bowlegs *hiepus* [went] with the white man—no come back'" (Dimmock 1908:312), referring to the Third Seminole War leader (Snake/Alligator Clan) who was emigrated to Oklahoma Territory in 1858. (Interestingly, the "old chief" refers to the same historic event that Charlie Osceola referred to in chapter 1. The forced emigration of Billy Bowlegs at the conclusion of the war had a great impact on the population of survivors and continued to do so for many decades to come.) Thus, the *i:laponathli:* felt great apprehension about leaving with non-Indians a situation that lasted through the first four decades of the twentieth century.

As a young man, W. Stanley Hanson, who would later be the closest advisor to the Big Cypress families, saw the economic advantages of their participation in events that would bolster their economy. In 1910 he tried to interest them in appearing under his supervision at the Panama Canal celebration in Tampa. His mother, Julia (1909), speculated that he would not succeed, noting, "These Seminoles are proud, reserved people, and I do not believe will consent to be made a show of."

An early exhibition that promoted the State of Florida opened March 24, 1924, at Madison Square Garden in snow-covered New York City.

Booths featured major cities with the theme "Everything here but the climate!" The exhibits were lavishly decorated with palms, orange trees, sugarcane, and Spanish moss. Fifty barefoot *i:laponathli:* accompanied this show in their colorful cotton clothing. The promoters had gotten off the train in Savannah and purchased overcoats for them, but they refused shoes (Hanna and Hanna 1948:335). The *New York Times* reported, "[The Seminoles] . . . saw snow for the first time in their lives when they arrived in NY yesterday, and they sat shivering around a gas stove, under a real coconut tree laden with matured fruit, in their booth at the Exhibition" (1924:12).

These families were from newly created Collier County in southwestern Florida and were representing it in one of its earliest promotional ventures. Barron Collier, founder of a national advertising franchise, who monopolized the county that bore his name, was on hand. Everglades promoter W. Guy Stovall was in charge of the *i:laponathli:* participants. He was an associate of Everglades promoter W. J. Conners, a major backer of the exhibition (ibid.; Hanna and Hanna 1948:335).

But during the engagement it appeared that the Florida Indians' subliminal fears of extradition might actually be realized: "After a dull day at the Garden some of the braves were taken on a sightseeing trip to Chinatown. In the course of the excursion they got their hands on some whiskey. . . . The effect was electric. Drunk as lords, they danced and yelled until some dumfounded Orientals called the police. This was momentarily sobering. What were the police going to do? asked one dancer to Stovall. 'Take you to Oklahoma,' snapped the exasperated chaperon who probably wished his charges were there already. What happened at that point transcended all previous activities, to borrow Stovall's description, 'It took about twelve cops to overcome each Indian.' The episode got into the papers and made the success of the exhibit" (Hanna and Hanna 1948:336).

It is not surprising that significant northern exhibitions featuring large Seminole village attractions were arranged and managed by Miami attraction personnel, whom the *i:laponathli:* participants knew well. Even so, it often took a great deal of persuasion to gain their confidence. These trips were demanding, up to seven months in length. Cold climates, absence from kinsmen who provided structure for the culture, and missing important socioreligious events such as the Green Corn Dance, were further drawbacks for the participants.

Seven years after the Madison Square Garden show and at the peak of the *i:laponathli:'* exhibition economy, the Miami and Miami Beach Chambers of Commerce teamed up to sponsor an exhibit for the 1931 Canadian National Exhibition in Toronto, billed as the "world's largest annual exhibition." The exhibit was arranged through the Florida and Canada Amusement Company of Miami Beach under promoters Max B. Kimmerer and Ross Young (Canadian National Exhibition 1931; Davis 1980). They produced shows throughout the 1930s, all of them successful. Their attention to details of the exhibits and careful selection of their personnel appear to have been contributing factors.

Coconut trees and other tropical plants, native animals, and a Seminole village were included in the exhibit (*Miami Daily News* 1931). The *Miami Herald* (1931) noted, "Bringing the American tropics to Canada naturally attracts favorable attention and the idea is an excellent one. It should turn the attention of our northern friends across the border to the possibilities of an enjoyable winter vacation."

Henry Coppinger, Jr., was contacted to arrange the Seminoles' participation. He was not sure that he could get any of the Indians to agree to go with him, but eventually he got some people interested. Once the word was out, it failed to meet the approval of other Indians in the city. Trouble brewed in what seems to have been a bout of rivalry tempered by a genuine concern about the welfare of those who would make the journey. A month before the Canadian party was to depart, word leaked out that Coppinger was taking Indians to Canada, and Henry was approached by a delegation from the Musa Isle Seminole Village. When Coppinger asked why they were so opposed to the trip, one man replied, "You have to skate around on skates . . . it's so cold!" Another asked, "What are they going to have to eat?" (Coppinger 1975).

Nonetheless, on July 29, 1931, all was ready for the journey. Boxcars had been loaded with entire coconut trees to be replanted in Toronto (*Miami Daily News* 1931). Over 30,000 palmetto fans had been cut and packed for the families to use to thatch five *chickees*. According to the *Official Catalogue*, the village was to be "reproduced as faithfully as if it had been picked up bodily from the heart of the Florida Everglades and moved in one piece to Toronto" (Coppinger Papers 1931a; Canadian National Exhibition 1931:43). An entire coach car had been reserved for the *i:laponathli:*, with the purchase of twenty-five tickets (Coppinger 1975).

Two weeks before the departure date Coppinger arranged for the twenty-three *i:laponathli:* to come to Miami and stay in the garden's village, closed during the off-season. Each family was paid $35 a week, plus food for the duration of the trip. Three sewing machines were rented for the women's use. Yard goods and thread were purchased: ninety yards of cambric, twelve of broadcloth, and twelve spools of number 30 thread (Coppinger Papers 1931b; Coppinger 1975).

L. Mike Osceola (Bird), a son of William McKinley Osceola, recalled that some of the Indians whom Coppinger had asked to go to Canada were seasonal employees of Musa Isle. Osceola thought that Bert Lasher doubtless wanted a commission per Indian (as they were *his* Indians), but Coppinger was not planning to pay him so Lasher decided to undermine Coppinger's plans. He took Charlie Billie (Wildcat), Conrad Billie (unidentified), and three or four other men across Biscayne Bay to the island of Key Biscayne, where he got them drunk and then left them. When they sobered up, they tried to get back to the mainland. They swam all the way across the bay, aided by a string of little islands and sandbars where they would stop and rest. Eventually they arrived in Miami, but they had missed the train (Osceola 1982).

On the morning of the scheduled departure, August 25, the promoters sent a truck to take the Canadian-bound Indians to the depot. Coppinger was astounded to find the village in disarray and no one stirring. He was told by the elderly headman John Osceola (Panther) that the Indians from Musa Isle had come to the camp at night and scared everyone about going to Canada. He thought quickly, as it was almost time for the train, and said to Osceola, "Let's you and me go. You're not scared!" Osceola agreed. As he got into the truck, his wife Ida (Otter) hurried out with her bundles, and everyone else followed. Coppinger told the driver not to stop for any lights, as he was afraid that some of the Indians might change their minds. When they boarded the day coach, Coppinger went as far as to tell the conductor to lock the doors. He was afraid that someone would bolt at the Fort Lauderdale or Palm Beach stops, but no one was so inclined (Coppinger 1975).

There were two crates of canned goods on the train as proof that no one would starve. Coppinger also packed meat, cheese, and ten loaves of bread. First-class meals were provided with their fare. The *Toronto Star Weekly* (1931) proclaimed, "Out from the jungle for the first time in history came families of a most ancient Mongol tribe!" Participating were John and Ida Osceola and their sixteen-year-old daughter, *Tihokee* (Otter), who had been recently married to Musa Isle's star alligator wrestler, Henry Cypress (Panther); Katie (Panther) and Josie Jumper (Bear) with their children Moses and Laura Mae; Katie's father, Sam Huff (Big Towns); and Chestnut Billie (Bird). It would appear that Lasher's plan to cripple Coppinger's tour did indeed cut the number of participants in half.

Five hundred alligators of various sizes, including eggs ready to hatch, were shipped to Canada, where Coppinger and his brother Jack put on the wrestling shows to the thrill of the Canadian crowds (*Toronto Star Weekly* 1931; *The Mail and Empire* 1931; Coppinger Papers 1931a).

Although the Canadian trip was well funded, some of the expo trips involving the Seminoles during the depression years were not. In 1932, Bert Lasher himself took *i:laponathli:* to a tourist attraction set up at Wildwood, New Jersey. A local newspaper advertised, "The Indians Are Coming!" (*Wildwood Leader* 1932). This show was evidently the brainchild of Henry Conant, a former mayor of Rehobeth, Maryland. According to the *Leader*, "Mr. Conant has spent the past winter in Miami with the interesting tribe and conceived the plan of bringing them north for the summer months. A force of mechanics are now at work rushing to complete the picturesque Seminole huts." This show seems to have been a low-budget endeavor: the structures were roofed with tree boughs rather than imported palmetto fans (Seminole/Miccosukee Photo Archive 1932a). Twenty-five *i:laponathli:* and six large alligators made the trip, and hourly alligator wrestling was featured. Lasher had recently gone bankrupt at Musa Isle, and he probably intended to recoup his losses with the Wildwood venture.

Meanwhile, on August 9, Henry Coppinger, Jr., was on tour with his alligator wrestling show and stopped in Wildwood. The Conant/Lasher show was apparently alluding to sponsorship from the Miami Chamber of Commerce. Guarding his business interests, Coppinger fired off a telegram to the chamber asking if they were in any way connected to this attraction. The reply: "We are not sponsoring or supporting any such business" (Coppinger Papers 1931c).

Regardless, the Wildwood attraction was a financial failure. The entrance fee on opening day in May was twenty-five cents for adults and fifteen for children, but by July the general admission had been reduced to ten cents (Boyer 1974). Josie Billie (Panther), a powerful medicine man, was the headman for this group. At the time, he was one of the most literate of the Florida Indians and an avid letter writer. On September 5, 1932, he wrote to his friend Capt. J. F. Jaudon, the builder of the Tamiami Trail, that the group would be leaving in a week, and he closed, "Tell Indians People Pretty soon Josie Billie he come back home Bring All Indians Back Home" (Billie 1932).

Risky low-budget shows like this one prompted Seminole agent James L. Glenn to condemn such ventures: "Some white man would get a group of Seminoles to go with him to exhibits and fairs throughout the nation. If he got enough money out of it, he would bring the Indians home. But if his business venture did not pay out he would desert them, and the U.S.I.S. [United States Indian Service] had to take over and finance enough of the venture to get the Indians back to Florida" (1982:106).

The Seminole Indian Association under Secretary W. Stanley Hanson interceded for the *i:laponathli:* in cases where their earnings had not been paid. Hanson wrote in his 1933–34 report, "At the request of Florida Indians correspondence was had with persons in Virginia who are due these Indians money, which it is hoped will soon be paid" (Hanson 1934).

Alan W. Davis took a group of *i:laponathli:* from Musa Isle to the Canadian National Exhibition in 1932, again under the sponsorship of Kimmerer and Young. With Davis in charge of the Seminoles, Henry Coppinger attended to his alligator wrestling shows. His good friend Phil James put on an archery show, and a high dive act was performed. South Florida flora and fauna were on display in the attraction called "The Seminole Village." The entrance to the village was flanked by huge palmetto-thatched pylons, and a raised platform supported the barkers. Posters and signs advertised "Seminole Indians" and Alligator Wrestling" (Canadian National Exhibition 1931:40; Seminole/Miccosukee Photo Archive 1932b; Davis 1980; James 1980). But, like Coppinger before him, Davis had experienced the *i:laponathli:'* lingering apprehension regarding the trip: "[It] was just too far away. They thought they might be sent to Oklahoma." Neither of Davis's closest *i:laponathli:* friends, Cory or William McKinley Osceola, would consider making the trip, "so," Davis related, "I had to go get Indians from way out in the 'Glades, very poor Indians" (Davis 1981a).

Josie Billie was the leader most agreeable to helping to recruit when *i:laponathli:* were contacted for promotional appearances. He was also Hanson's closest confidant. Earlier, in 1928, Hanson was asked to hire some Seminoles to attend the opening ceremonies for the Tamiami Trail. His correspondence with the sponsor shows the persistent strength of the traditional leadership: "Seminoles agreeable to trip but in absence of their Medicine Man [Josie Billie] can make no final decision now."

Davis hired Josie Billie and William McKinley Osceola to recruit Indians for the Canadian trip. They went west from Miami by truck on the Tamiami Trail, then turned north on boggy trails that took them about twenty miles into the Big Cypress. Billie and Osceola felt that the Big Cypress people would benefit financially from this endeavor. Davis recalled that these *i:laponathli:* "didn't have [anything]." He brought them back to Musa Isle and, with the promoters' backing, fed them and gave them material for clothing: "[It] took me a month to get them fixed up."

Some of those who had been on earlier northern excursions were also hired. Doubtless they provided some assurance to the new recruits. Davis drove the twenty-seven Indians to Toronto in an old schoolbus. At night they camped along the highway, cooked over their traditional fire, and slept in the woods (Davis 1980, 1981a). Frank Willie (Bird) told his nephew, Mike Osceola (1982), that they had fun on the road. They could not read maps, but at night when they camped and someone would ask "Which way's Miami? Which way's home?" Willie would look up at the stars and, with the navigator's knowledge that *i:laponathli:* canoemen retained at the time, would point "There!" During Davis's promotional ventures as the manager for participating *i:laponathli:*, he looked to headman William McKinley Osceola as his contact on issues dealing with the welfare of these Native Americans. Their friendship and the feasibility of a telephone call or telegram reaching Osceola at Musa Isle (later at Osceola's Gardens and Osceola's Indian Village) in Miami made him an important contact.

Participants Katie and Josie Jumper, who had attended the 1931 show, returned in 1932 (Laura Mae Osceola 1991). Sisters Mary and Ruby Tiger (Panther) with their uncle Joe Henry Tiger (Panther) (Mary Tiger 1982); Homespun Billie (Otter); the Johnny Busters with children Junior and Mary (Wildcat) and Sally Johns (Wildcat) were also on this trip (Jimmie O. Osceola 1991; L. Mike Osceola 1982).

At the Canadian Exposition representatives from the State Fair of Texas invited the Kimmerer/Young show to Dallas for two weeks on their return trip to Miami. Davis wrote William McKinley Osceola for permission, which he granted. All of the *chickees* were dismantled, and the palmettos were repacked and shipped to be reconstructed in Dallas where the show ran October 8–23 (Davis 1980).

Based on the success of the Canadian shows, a third Kimmerer/Young exhibition opened at the Century of Progress in Chicago in 1933. This event ran from May 27 through November 13, the longest one thus far for the participating *i:laponathli:*. Alan Davis returned as producer and manager of the Indian village. All additional events that had proved so successful remained the same. Banana plants and coconut trees were again shipped by train to landscape the village, but this tour was so long that the trees died. A painter was hired to spray them green.

It was not an easy job to make a home away from home for the *i:laponathli:*, but it appears that Davis did his best. While the fairgoers could see the women sewing, working on crafts in the five *chickees*, and cooking over their traditional star fires, Davis partitioned off their eating area for privacy. Foodstuffs were purchased in bulk, but he ran into a problem when he tried to locate a supplier of "grits," finely ground corn, for making the Seminole staple *o'they* (*sofki*). Unable to find a source of this decidedly southern staple in the Windy City, he finally placed an order with a distributor in Louisville, Kentucky, for 100-pound sacks (Davis 1980).

Some of the seasoned participants at this show were the Johnny Busters with their children, Junior and Mary and Sally Johns; Katie and Josie Jumper and their children, Moses and Laura Mae. Other employees were George Osceola (Deer), Chestnut Billie (Bird), and Josie Billie. But even though they were getting $50 a week, participants found this tour too long. Late in the engagement, some employees wanted to leave. Davis told them, "No, we've got so many more weeks. We're all together. Let's fight it out" (Jimmie O. Osceola 1991; L. Mike Osceola 1982). One man in the group had a drinking problem. Davis did not want him to be picked up by the local police, so he constructed a small palmetto thatched jail where he could sober up. "He could have come out of there if he'd wanted to," Davis recalled (1981a). The typical *i:laponathli:'* method of dealing with drunkenness was to immobilize the person by tying his hands and feet and leaving him to sober up.

Alligator wrestling was the responsibility of Josie Jumper and Chestnut Billie. They received salaries but alternated shows in order to even out tips. Non-Indian employees Phil Wofford and Tex Farless of Musa Isle were also hired for village duties and as occasional alligator wrestlers (Davis 1980). The weekly feeding of the alligators, so popular with spectators, took place on Friday afternoons. The attraction was often so crowded that no one could move. Admission to the village was twenty-five cents. The Chicago World's Fair attracted 22.3 million persons in five and a half months (*Miami Herald* 1933).

Information from Florida was welcomed by the homesick *i:laponathli:*. Hanson wrote in his 1933–34 report, "The Seminoles attending the Chicago World's Fair were kept informed regarding their folks back in Florida by your secretary, and reports received from there time to time, which were communicated to the Florida Indians."

When Alan W. Davis lectured in Chicago on the life-style of the Seminole, he usually asked two adults and the village children to stand with him. In this era of hype, the audience was skeptical of his assessment of their life-style. When Davis was discussing the rituals of the Green Corn Dance, their major religious event, he described the "scratching" of all the males with needles. A professor from a local university spoke up and said, "Mister, that was done maybe a good many years ago, but why try and fool us by telling us that they do that today?" As it so happened Josie Billie was on this tour. Several weeks before, he had conducted an abbreviated Corn Dance for the *i:laponathli:* at the Chicago event. Davis asked Josie Jumper, the alligator wrestler, to remove his shirt. There were the long scratch marks, made by needles, healing on his body (Davis 1981a).

The final Kimmerer/Young tour opened at the New York World's Fair in 1939. The duration of this show was a grueling seven months (ibid.). The fifty *i:laponathli:* arrived in New York early in the morning on April 18. Davis recalled the picture they made sitting in a circle on the marble floor in the middle of Penn Station eating their breakfast (*Okeechobee News* 1939; Davis 1980).

It was cold in New York. When they reached the village, the unknowing workmen had built the *chickee* platforms six inches off the ground like a floor, rather than the elevated platform that the Seminoles would sit on while hanging their feet over the side. The group had to make a temporary camp in one of the Fair buildings while the carpenters were recalled (Davis 1980; *New York Times* 1939). The largest sizes of tennis shoes were ordered for the women who were unaccustomed to shoes, while heavy canvas was purchased to enclose three sides of the five *chickees* where heaters were installed. Despite these efforts, a four-month-old baby was hospitalized with pneumonia (Davis 1980). The cold also had detrimental effects on the imported coconut trees and a fatal effect on the crocodiles, but the alligators endured.

The large Kimmerer/Young shows featuring a full-scale Seminole village were prototypes for smaller tourist shows that often traveled with carnivals. These shows usually featured animals, high-dive exhibitions, and a single *i:laponi:* family who brought an alligator for the ever popular wrestling act. In 1937, L. Mike Osceola, Johnny Tigertail (Big Towns), and Katie Jumper and her children toured the eastern states with the All American Carnival operated by Joe and Edith Russo (Guttman 1982; L. Mike Osceola 1982). The economic benefits of tourism occasionally reached up the coast to the *ci:saponathli:* camps east of Lake Okeechobee. In 1935 nineteen members of a Fort Pierce area camp were featured at an attraction in Lake Ariel, Pennsylvania *(Tallahassee Democrat* 1935).

A few writers attempted to explore the influence of these trips on the participants. Folklorist Robert F. Greenlee noted in 1944, "Some Seminoles have visited cities far removed from their local habitat and this has led to further acculturation at home." Speaking of his major contact, the inquisitive Josie Billie, Greenlee commented, "Travel has made him more worldly-wise than some of his fellows" (1952:28). Anthropologist James O. Buswell's opinion on this process concluded, "When an entertainment or exhibition contact community would be established . . . the impact upon those Indians participating would be more lasting, since it presumably increased aspirations toward the external system in some cases, primarily among the men, and increased dissatisfactions with their own system in certain respects upon their return" (1972:335–36).

However, on the basis of my study, *i:laponathli:* participants were not changed by their experiences outside of their own environment, perhaps because they carried with them the strict mores of their culture and the solidarity of the *i:laponathli:* camp so touted by Spoehr (1941:13–14). Indeed, the exhibition tours to northern cities appear to have been looked on as little more than just another job.

CHAPTER 9

Media Chiefs, Politicians, and Councilmen

Let us alone.

i:laponathli: council (1936), Cory Osceola, interpreter

The headman in the Seminole village tourist attraction was a visible fig-urehead in that small *i:laponathli:* community and was treated as such by the attraction owners and operators. He was the liaison with the media, dealing with reporters, writers, and federal men on behalf of the attraction or, more important, the *i:laponathli:*. In the stereotypical view that "all Indians have chiefs," this spokesman was dubbed "chief" by the tourists and the media, but, of course, he was not. The headman, then, had a great responsibility, as the tourist attraction placed him in an artificial position of authority over the entire *i:laponathli:* population, along with his paying job (West 1981:205). It was an abuse of this position that led to a test of the *i:laponathli:'* latent concept of their sovereignty.

The startling results of the Drainage Commission's policies and the land boom they created gave way to a number of novel celebrations in southeastern Florida. In early 1927, the Miami Chamber of Commerce formulated plans for festivities that they hoped would make national news. They were celebrating not only the creation of new land from the Everglades but also the resultant emergence of two new towns, Opa Locka and Hialeah. *Reclamation* was the word of the day, as canals, ditches, dikes, and new roads crisscrossed lands recently under water. The Chamber established a prestigious Everglades Committee under Ernest R. Graham to promote sales of former Everglades land.

The resulting "Forward to the Soil" production was held near Hialeah on the Roselawn Tract, 150,000 acres of reclaimed land. A well-staged publicity stunt, the event, it was hoped, would "give impetus" to the Chamber's campaign to promote and sell land while also furnishing "photographic copy for advertising Miami's reclamation program throughout the country" (*Miami Daily News* 1927). The *Miami Herald* (1927) noted, "All of these ceremonies and events will be filmed by newsreel cameramen, these having assured the committee of their presence, because of the historical and national interest in the event." Rufus Steele, whose occupation was magazine editor, headed the production's committee, and it was under his direction. The key participants in this event were the Seminoles.

On the high and now dry Hialeah Prairie, February 5, 1927, was a sunny day. A traditional cooking *chickee* had been erected, and a speakers' platform stood nearby. Soon, twenty Indians, city officials, newsmen, and a crowd of 5,000 spectators had gathered. The theme of the day was stated in the official program: "The Seminole Indians Ancient Masters of the Everglades Surrender The Sovereignty Of The Muck Lands To Their Palefaced Brothers" (Miami Chamber of Commerce 1927).

Tony Tommie (Panther), headman at Musa Isle, played a prominent role in this production. A *ci:saponi:*, in 1915 he had been the first Seminole to attend formal public school in Fort Lauderdale (McGoun 1972:48). As an adult, his literacy gained him a key position at the Musa Isle tourist attraction, where he was dubbed Chief of the Seminoles by the media. But he abused his acquired status by not consulting the council. He then placed himself at odds with the Seminole Agency and its programs, causing special commissioner Lucien A. Spencer to dub him a "self-styled chief" (Nash 1931:25).

Tommie's address was read by Miami Chamber member Charles H. Hessler from a transcription: "The Great Spirit has troubled our minds in these latter days and we have harkened to the Voice. The Child of Nature must allow the child of Destiny his way. Thus we have made our tribal peace with the White Father in Washington. Thus yield we willingly into your eager hands the mastery of the raven-black soil. Foreseen by us and understood by us is the change that now will come when the white man has his way" (Miami Chamber of Commerce 1927).

Chamber president Lon Worth Crow's address reiterated the fact that "peace" had been made: "Two moons ago, you made your peace with the white father in Washington, and brought officially to an end that ancient feud between your ancestors and our ancestors, which could have no place in the new Florida, where at last men view each other with eyes unveiled. In thus entreating peace with the Federal Government, you evoked blessing upon your people, and my people, and upon all men. It is fitting therefore, that we thus publicly and solemnly commemorate the delivery by you and the acceptance by us, of a responsibility so great" (ibid.).

It was on November 26, 1926, that "Chief Tony Tommie" announced at a press conference that "the Indians have decided to ask for citizenship in the United States and to swear their allegiance to America." He told reporters that he had sent a letter to President Calvin Coolidge to that effect, which was relative to discussions he had with officials when he was in Washington earlier in the year. "He added that he intends to call a general council of the men in the Everglades in the near future to discuss developments in connection with their step towards allegiance." It was also stated that "he had made the decision without a recent conclave of braves" and that he had sent the letter to the president "after a conference with Miami attorneys engaged to assist him" (*Miami Herald* 1926c).

Thus, two months prior to Forward to the Soil, Tommie had "made peace with the White Father at Washington." In all fairness, few whites understood the workings of the traditional political system. To the great majority of Miamians (most of them new arrivals), to the media, and to the tourists, Tony Tommie was obviously the chief of the Seminoles who could make peace if he so wanted. However, he was not, and this publicity stunt, coupled with the audacity of the production's script, came to the attention of the *i:laponathli:* council, the governing body.

Until this time, there had been little need for the council to address the tangibility of their concept of sovereignty, but the possible ramifications of Tommie's actions as they might be viewed by the government were catastrophic. This event was seen as a direct threat to the *i:laponathli:* way of life, one that could undercut their own autonomous position and rights (West 1992a).

The Indian contingency included Tony Tommie's *ci:saponathli:* mother and uncle. *I:laponathli:* Cory Osceola (whom Annie Tommie had raised as her own son) was probably an unwitting player in this production, and he doubtless later regretted it. However, it also seems apparent that prior to the production, the Indian participants were not aware of the significance of the symbolic role they would be acting out. They were accustomed to being booked for a diversity of local events and doubtless considered this one to be just another gig that Bert Lasher got for them which would bring them extra pay.

During the ceremonies they performed their prescribed roles: "Offering of Muck Soil Vegetables and Fruits by Seminole Braves and Squaws in Procession"; "The Seminole Chieftain and Braves Cut and Set Up a Cake of Muck Soil"; "Braves Send a Shower of Peace Arrows into the Everglades"; "Braves Illustrate the Use of Their Tribal Wooden Spades, and Squaws Sow the Corn as It Has Been Sown in the Everglades for Two Hundred Years." They also performed two dances from the Green Corn Dance, which Steel described to the press as "colorful, hilarious, and picturesque" (*Miami Herald* 1927). Representing local state "Society Queens," scantily clad "Farmerettes" led by "Miss Miami" and modern-day tractors contrasted with the traditionally clad Indians with their simple but effective planting methods.

A special ceremony was to conclude peace between the Seminoles and the whites and also to transfer the Seminoles' rights to the Everglades lands to their "white brothers." The program described this event: "The Peace Pipe Smoked When the Blackfeet Made a Treaty with the United States Government Is Lighted from the Council Fire, and Chief Tony Tommie and [Chamber] President Lon Worth Crow Smoke a Pipe of Peace, Thus Cementing the Red Man and the White Man in Solemn and Irrevocable Agreement over the Agricultural Lands of the Everglades" (Miami Chamber of Commerce 1927). The peace pipe was the property of Rufus Steele, who was considered an authority on Native Americans. He assured the press that "once a pact is cemented by the smoking of this pipe of peace the sovereignty of the Florida Everglades passes from the Seminole Indians into the hands of the white man" (*Miami Herald* 1927). The peace pipe, bows and arrows, and a Plains Indian bonnet of eagle feathers that Tony Tommie wore in the ceremony were of course commoditizing elements of the white man's stereotypical image of "The American Indian."

The *Miami Daily News*, a great supporter of the Seminole, frequently published news concerning their special events and obituaries and highlighting their culture or conditions in feature articles and series. With its history of treating the *i:laponathli:* with dignity, the paper candidly observed of the ceremony, "Tony Tommie and his band of Seminoles . . . performed roles of subservience under the direction of Rufus Steele" (1927). But theirs was a small voice of opposition to the Miami Chamber's grandiose farce.

Miami's top three photographers—Claude C. Matlack, Gleason Waite Romer, and Frank A. Robinson—were on hand to document the ceremony. Images taken in sequence by Romer, photographer for the *Miami News*, depict a Seminole flag flying (Romer 1927). It had horizontal stripes of yellow, red, black, and white, representing the four directions, known as the "medicine colors." The flag was obviously fabricated for this occasion and thus was flown for the first time. (I have not seen earlier photos of such a flag or found any earlier mention of flags in the literature or in the photographic record.) As the spectators and the mixed group of *i:laponathli:* and *ci:saponathli:* looked on, there was an exchange of flags, and the "Seminole" flag was replaced by the Stars and Stripes. Young Cory Osceola had the dubious honor of bringing down the "Seminole" flag.

Just ten days after the February 5 production of Forward to the Soil, the *St. Petersburg Daily News* ran an article with the headline "Seminole Chief Denounces Tony Tommie as 'Fakir and Traitor'." The article contained a letter from Ingraham Billie (Panther), a high-ranking councilman. He had contacted his brother, Josie Billie, who in turn contacted their associate W. Stanley Hanson. Billie instructed Hanson to send an urgent letter to Senator Duncan U. Fletcher, a member of the U.S. Senate Committee on Indian Affairs. Hanson wrote to Fletcher for Billie:

> I am asked to say to you that Hath-wa-ha-chee (Tony Tommy) of Miami, who terms himself "Chief Tony Tommy" has no right to make any arrangements whatever concerning the Seminoles in Florida; is not a member of the Indian council; is not a chief of the Seminoles and never has been. Tony Tommy is seeking newspaper publicity for his own financial gain, greatly to the displeasure of the other Florida Indians, who absolutely ignore his statements.
>
> In fairness to our Indians will you please see that the Commissioner of Indian Affairs is acquainted with these facts, and let the commissioner know that our Indians repudiate "Chief" Tony

Tommy and his actions and trust the commissioner will pay no attention whatsoever to the self-styled "Chief" Tony Tommy.

These facts have been duly made known to Capt. L. A. Spencer, U.S. agent for the Seminoles in Florida, who is aware that Tony Tommy is a full fledged fakir.

With kind personal wishes to you believe me always
Very respectfully yours
W. Stanley Hanson, Secretary
Seminole Indian Association
(*St. Petersburg Daily News* 1927; Hanson 1927).

Senator Fletcher replied to Hanson that his letter would be submitted to the Department of the Interior Office of Indian Affairs. He also commented, "It is my understanding that Mr. Spencer, when here a few weeks ago, advised Commissioner Burke [of Indian Affairs] regarding Tony Tommie's lack of responsibility" (Fletcher 1927).

Bert Lasher appears to have asked a friend, Miami attorney O. B. White, in 1927 to advise the *i:laponathli:*, doubtless as a result of Forward to the Soil (Davis 1980). White remained their pro bono legal council for the next twenty-seven years (U.S. Congress 1954:1133). By 1939, he was signing documents as "Attorney for the Seminole Nation" (*American Eagle* 1935; Stipulation 1939). Cory and Juanita Osceola named one of their sons O. B. White Osceola (Panther) in honor of their long-time friendship with the lawyer.

More and more the *i:laponathli:* were sought out by the media. An important elder councilman such as Cuffney Tiger, Josie Billie, or Ingraham Billie might be interviewed for an opinion or, following the advice of white associates, might make a statement, but Cory Osceola, the new headman and media spokesman for Musa Isle, fielded most questions directed to the council. While he too was dubbed "chief" by the press, it appears that, unlike Tommie, he complied with the wishes of the council, acting in his best capacity as a watchdog for the nonreservation *i:laponathli:*. His son, O. B. White Osceola, Sr., reflected, "My Dad, he always says he's 'Interpreter.' People call him Chief. Everybody knows what he does" (1985). Cory Osceola continued this watchful role until his death in 1979 (West 1987b).

The headman of the tourist attraction was in a unique political position. Because he was bilingual and literate, the tourist attraction hierarchy considered this man the "smartest" of the lot. Besides media liaison, the headman's duties included not only the recruitment of Indian employees but the handling of grocery money, granting and dispensing salaries, and keeping order. The head men commanded a special salary (Dade County Chancery Records 1932; Davis 1980). Headmen at Coppinger's/Pirate's Cove between 1918 and 1940 were Jack Tiger Tail (Wind; wife, Big Towns); Charlie Billie (Wildcat; wife, Bird); and John Osceola (Panther; wife, Otter). At Musa Isle, headmen were Willie Willie (Bird), Tony Tommie (Panther; wife, Big Towns); Cory Osceola (Big Towns; wife, Panther); and William McKinley Osceola (Big Towns; wife, Bird).

Cory Osceola was the first leader to come from the tourist attraction pool who lent his skills of leadership both to the attractions and to the *i:laponathli:* council. He was aware of situations as soon as they occurred and handled them with the council's approval. His working relationship with White provided the legal background for his responses. In 1930, for instance, Cory Osceola sent a telegram to President Herbert Hoover reprimanding him for appointing an Oklahoma Seminole, "Chili Fish, as principal chief of the 'Seminole Nation,' for a day to act for the Indians in a proposed land transfer." It was not clear whether this transfer would affect the Seminoles in Florida, but taking no chances Osceola stated their position: "We are satisfied with our homes in the Everglades. Our forefathers held this land against the white man and we have lived on it ever since. We do not agree to anything but to be let alone in possession of Florida from which white men failed to drive us" (*Miami Daily News* 1930c).

Tony Tommie was diagnosed with tuberculosis soon after "Forward to the Soil" and left Florida for a sanatorium in Oklahoma. It was in 1930 that Tony Tommie returned from Oklahoma and attempted to usurp Cory Osceola's authority. But Tommie found himself unwelcome and thus did not resume his position as headman of Musa Isle (*Miami Daily News* 1930b). Little wonder that Tommie felt that "medicine men were fixing medicine on him and he doesn't think he's going to live" (Juanita Osceola 1985). Tommie succumbed to tuberculosis on April 6, 1931 (Oliver 1931).

In 1935, another threat to their sovereignty was perceived by the *i:laponathli:* council, this time from reservation Indians who, like Tommie, were *ci:saponathli:*. By 1928 only a small percentage of the Florida Seminole population lived on the newly created Dania Reservation; most of the residents were *ci:saponathli:*, while the *i:laponathli:* population generally kept their distance.

Some of the reservation population had come from Annie Tommie's (Panther) Fort Lauderdale camp, which was being threatened by white encroachment. Others—including the relations of Mary Tustenuggee (Mrs. Capt. Tom) Tiger, her daughter Ada, and brother Jimmie Gopher—had been transported south from the Indiantown Snake Clan camp near Lake Okeechobee. Both of these families were half Creek, half *i:laponathli:*, and, as mentioned, they were considered by south Florida's *i:laponathli:* majority to be "different" from them (Sturtevant 1956:58; King 1978:152–56, 160). One *i:laponi:* man offered, "White people could influence Creeks much easier" (King 1978:153).

Perhaps that is what they thought when Ivy Stranahan of Fort Lauderdale persuaded Annie Tommie's family to be the first residents on the new Dania Reservation in 1926. Then Mary Tiger's family (Snake Clan) arrived. This family had the distinction (and the stigma) of being the first Seminole Christian converts. Because they had converted, they had been treated as outcasts in the northern community. Ada Tiger sold her sizable cattle interests in 1927 to move south to the Dania Reservation, where the lives of her two half-white children would no longer be threatened by the *ci:saponathli:* councilmen (West 1995b). But Lucien Spencer, special commissioner to the Seminole, perhaps attempting to garner commendation for his zeal in carrying out his directive to establish a reservation school, stated in his annual report that he starved Ada Tiger's family by cutting off government rations in order to gain her children as statistics for the school (Department of the Interior 1927:7). One might ask how he starved out a cattle baroness, but the children were the impetus for the Tigers' significant move south to the reservation.

The establishment of a *ci:saponathli:* enclave on the federal reservation, with Christian converts as well, colored the already anti-reservation, anti-government, anti-*ci:saponathli:* mindset of the *i:laponathli:* population. L. Mike Osceola was an early acculturated *i:laponathli:*, a child reared at Musa Isle Seminole Village, who was to become involved in the politics of Seminole tribal formation in the 1950s. He noted in a 1982 interview that much of the *i:laponathli:* resentment of the *ci:saponathli:* had died out by then. He explained that the *i:laponathli:'* ill feelings toward the "Creeks" went back to before the Second Seminole War, when some *ci:saponathli:* agreed to sell their cattle and move to the Indian Territory. Yet, he noted that since that time, the *i:laponathli:* "never trusted the Creeks fully."

Special Commissioner James L. Glenn was the one catering to the interests of a handful of *ci:saponathli:* who wished to ask the federal government for concessions under the provisions of the Wheeler-Howard Bill, the Indian Reorganization Act. Sam Tommie (the brother of the late

Tony Tommie) resided at that time on the Dania Reservation (now Hollywood). He had married a *ci:saponathli:* from the Cow Creek camps east of Lake Okeechobee. But in this matrilineal society, Mildred Bowers Tommie (Bird) had no reservation within her families' settlement area. Thus, Sam Tommie became the one who spoke for the few northern *ci:saponathli:* willing to be the first Florida Seminoles to establish relations with the government and ask for concessions.

A historic meeting was arranged between the *ci:saponathli:* (represented by Glenn and Tommie) and representatives from the U.S. Indian Service. Unfortunately, in order to assure a large Seminole contingency, it was scheduled to be held at the West Palm Beach Sun Dance Festival, which had been attended annually since 1916 by both *ci:saponathli:* and *i:laponathli:* families.

Although the atmosphere of the festival was informal, the meeting was to be significant. In fact, it was truly the first formal meeting of the Seminoles with U.S. officials since war times. The media saw this, obviously, as a "peace conference." The headline in the *Miami Herald* (1935), "End of 100-Year War of Seminoles Nearing," was followed by this story: "The Seminoles' petition which will be presented to Secretary Ickes and Commissioner Collier, asked for 'all rights and privileges of citizens and a grant of 200,000 acres of land in the Glades.' Furthermore, explains Sam Tommie, [erroneously identified as] spokesman for the medicine men of the tribe, the Seminoles want $15.00 per capita per month upon the promise that they will swear allegiance to the United States."

Even federal Indian Commissioner John Collier felt that the meeting would "conclude a kind of treaty of peace between the United States Government and the Seminoles and to bring them into our Indian efforts" (Glenn 1982:63). Little wonder then, that the *New York Times* also reported to the country, "Florida's Seminole Indians after 100 years of technical warfare with the United States plan to offer the pipe of peace" (1935).

According to Glenn's memoirs, Cory Osceola and his brother William McKinley Osceola, on hearing of the proposed conference, got the message out to Sam Tommie (Panther) and other participants that anyone signing the New Deal document would be killed (Glenn 1976:4). However, when questioned about this sensational proclamation years later, Cory Osceola's widow felt that Cory Osceola "won't use that word!" She suggested that it was probably a rumor started by Sam Tommie (Juanita Osceola 1985). Bert Lasher was also against the *i:laponathli:'* participation in the conference and persuaded the "20 or more" Indians from Miami not to attend (Burghard 1935).

However, the *i:laponathli:* council's response to the conference was immediate. Under the caption "Big Cypress Indians Aroused," they put together a press release with attorney White's aid: "We, the chiefs, leaders, medicine men, being the duly constituted authority to speak for and on behalf of the true Seminole Indians who live in the Big Cypress Country in Western Dade, Northern Monroe, Eastern Collier, Southern Lee and Hendry Counties, in the southern portion of the State of Florida, desiring to voice the protest of our people and, after consultation with the members of our tribes, desire to call attention of the Indian Commissioner to the fact that the Seminoles are not at peace and have never signed any peace treaty with the United States of America" (*American Eagle* 1935).

This conference, as it affected the *i:laponathli:*, could be seen as similar to other examples of U.S. treaty making with Native Americans. Wilcomb E. Washburn, a historian who specializes in Indian-white relations, commented on U.S.–Native American treaty making in the nineteenth century: "Too frequently treaties were negotiated with one portion of the tribe and rejected by another portion. With the signature of some Indians on the document, American negotiators usually discounted the opposition of the non-signers" (1975:100).

This description certainly applied to the West Palm Beach conference. Prior to the event, attorney O. B. White had written Florida Senator J. Mark Wilcox "to protest that the secretary and commissioner would be meeting with a hand-picked group of Indians who did not represent the views of the entire tribe" (Kersey 1989:84). In all fairness, Glenn had met with some of the *i:laponathli:* opposed to the conference (presumably the Osceola brothers) and arranged to have trucks pick them up in Miami and take them to West Palm Beach so that their views could be heard. But Lasher and the Osceolas opposed this idea, the latter because they had not called the conference themselves and did not want to jeopardize their antigovernment position by meeting with government representatives.

Upon his return to Washington, Secretary Ickes felt in his own defense (as he had not received the White-Wilcox correspondence prior to leaving Washington) that the Indians at the conference "were fairly representative," and he believed "that the Indians who spoke at West Palm Beach voiced the real wishes of most Seminoles" (Kersey 1989:84). But while having no voice at the West Palm Beach conference, the *i:laponathli:* councilmen's threatening message to all of the Florida Seminoles carried a lot of weight. To the amazement of the Washington officials, there were indeed *no* Indian signatures on the petition presented to U.S. Indian Commissioner John Collier (Glenn 1976:4).

Calling the government's West Palm Beach conference a publicity stunt, the thrust of the council's protest was the Wheeler-Howard Bill itself. According to its stipulations, Indians living under government supervision could organize and govern themselves and would then receive economic opportunities. During a heated council meeting in Big Cypress, the *i:laponathli:* leaders in consultation with White decided that since their own group was "free and independent" of the government, a delegation of six men would go to Miami and sign a formal affidavit "protesting for their tribe against the Wheeler-Howard Bill. The affidavit expressly requested the Committee on Indian Affairs to exempt the Big Cypress country of South Florida from the operation and effects of the bill" (*American Eagle* 1935). The *i:laponathli:* councilmen claimed that the reservation lands were poor hunting grounds and that a state of war continued to exist between themselves and the government. They rejected the *ci:saponi:*' leader's plea for "all rights and privileges of citizens," and they claimed the whole of Florida as their land. The affidavit was signed by Cory Osceola (Big Towns), William McKinley Osceola (Big Towns), Richard Osceola (Bird) (a *ci:saponi:* married to an *i:laponi:*), Charlie Billie (Wildcat), Josie Billie (Panther), and Chestnut Billie (Bird) (ibid.). Special Commissioner James L. Glenn bitterly discussed Bert Lasher's (or perhaps legal council O. B. White's) manipulative role to keep the *i:laponathli:* from the Government's programs.

> . . . Certain self appointed "guardians" of the tribe became greatly excited . . . lest the "poor Indians" were about to be tricked. Municipal rivalry projected itself into the occasion, and made a show of child-like conduct. Predatory interests were aroused. The management of one of the commercial Indian villages expressed the opinion that the proposed conference was a foolish move on the part of the people of Florida. For, if the Indians in this conference manifested a friendship for the Government and if the press of the nation published this fact, the tourist would lose interest in seeing him and the trade which had grown out of this interest would be lost. All of these agencies conspired to embitter the Indians toward the conference and frighten them from it thereby to lead them to retain the reputation as enemies of the American Government. (Department of the Interior 1935:8)

It seems puzzling that Lasher—who allowed Musa Isle Indians' participation in the "Forward to the Soil" ceremonies (in 1927)—would be so adamant in persuading them against such activities in 1935. Perhaps White had opened Lasher's eyes to the *i:laponathli:* council's viewpoint.

Hanson continued to aid the *i:laponathli:* by organizing trips that provided them economic benefits. On one such excursion on December 28, 1935, they attended the commemoration at Bushnell, Florida, of the 100th anniversary of the initial battle of the Second Seminole War, called the Dade Battle or the Dade Massacre. There, the forty *i:laponathli:* made the acquaintance of Governor David Sholtz. Having met him face to face in an informal and casual atmosphere the *i:laponathli:* elders were most cordial.

Sholtz visited them in the southern Everglades on February 22, 1936. Cory Osceola served as spokesman for the elderly senior councilman, Dr. Tiger (Panther). As might be expected, this meeting, the first in which the reticent *i:laponathli:* had agreed to meet with government officials since the nineteenth century, generated a great deal of publicity. The *i:laponathli:* were still cautious and had with them their two most trusted advisors, W. Stanley Hanson and O. B. White. Hanson has been credited with organizing the historic meeting (*American Eagle* 1936). Hanson and White were asked to remain during the actual conference when the press was asked to leave the area. Governor Sholtz asked what he could do to help the Seminole. Cory Osceola replied for the councilmen, "They want to be left alone. They are afraid they will again be moved from the villages which they occupy deep in the Everglades. They fear the white men will keep on moving them until they are in the water. That was the expression they used" (Hanson 1936).

Doubtless the governor was chagrined at so unexpected and poignant a reply. He had seen this conference as a publicity stunt of his own to garner political clout. His visit was to call attention to the resourceful manner in which the State of Florida had exchanged, with the federal government, Indian lands for the huge acreage of Everglades National Park while gaining even greater acreage north of the Tamiami Trail for the state's new Indian reservation (Kersey 1989:109). For the *i:laponathli:*, however, Sholtz and the government cost them an excellent hunting area from which they were forcibly banned as early as June 1936 (*Homestead Enterprise* 1936).

In 1939, sovereignty continued to be an issue of concern to the seemingly overcautious *i:laponathli:* leaders and their attorney. There had not been a major northern exhibition with Seminole participation since the Chicago Exposition in 1933, but in 1939 a Seminole village was to be erected at the New York World's Fair and, they were told, President Franklin D. Roosevelt himself was to tour the fair.

Activist William McKinley Osceola (Big Towns) was head of Bert Lasher's Osceola's Indian Village on the Miami Canal. Under the title "spokesman and counselor to the Seminole Nation," he had White draw up a legal document that prohibited the signing of a peace treaty! This document, in the form of a stipulation, was prepared in White's office. It is a rare artifact of *i:laponathli:* sovereignty which stated in part that the participants at the fair would not "sign or consent to or make any agreement with the Government of the United States of America, or any of its representatives, or agents, or to subject the Seminole Nation, either expressly or by implication in any wise in any manner pertaining to the affairs of the Seminole Nation in its relation or non relation to the Government of the United States of America" (Stipulation 1939).

The *i:laponathli:* had learned a valuable lesson from Forward to the Soil. They realized that in their tenuous position—having no land that was legally their own, wanting no aid from the federal government, yet proudly asserting their "unconquered" status—their future rights could indeed be jeopardized by the actions of people who did not live by the traditional council's wishes. They realized that they must protect themselves to assure their future and their sovereignty.

Above: 1. A bus with *i:laponathli:* passengers promoting both Willie Willie's Indian Village at Musa Isle and the town of Hialeah in northwest Miami, Hialeah, 1922. William A. Fishbaugh, photographer. By permission of the Florida State Archives, Tallahassee.

Left: 2. Willie Willie (Bird Clan), December 11, 1923. He constructed the first Seminole Indian village at Musa Isle (ca. 1919) and operated the attraction on the property owned by John A. Roop. He was also a mannequin for Burdine's Department Store in downtown Miami. Claude C. Matlack, photographer. By permission of the Historical Museum of Southern Florida, Miami, no. 92-30.

Left: 3. Jack Tiger Tail (Wind Clan), 1920. Photo made for the town of Hialeah publicity campaign. R. W. Harrison Photographic Studio, Miami. By permission of the Seminole/ Miccosukee Photographic Archive, Fort Lauderdale, no. 403.

Below: 4. Billboard advertisement of Jack Tiger Tail at the town of Hialeah, 1921. William A. Fishbaugh, photographer. By permission of the Florida State Archives, Tallahassee, no. x340.

Above: 5. Coppinger's Tropical Gardens and Pirate's Cove, the earliest Seminole Indian Village tourist attraction, Miami, ca. 1921. By permission of the Seminole/Miccosukee Photographic Archive, Fort Lauderdale, no. 169.

Left: 6. Henry Coppinger, Jr., who commercialized the sport of alligator wrestling, 1921. By permission of the Seminole/Miccosukee Photographic Archive, Fort Lauderdale, no. 170.

Above: 7. A view of Musa Isle Seminole Indian Village fronting on the Miami River, ca. 1928, showing thatched dwelling *chickees* and, in the center, two cooking *chickees*, with alligator pens and wrestling pit in the background. By permission of the Seminole/Miccosukee Photographic Archive, Fort Lauderdale, no. 95.2.18.

Left: 8. Egbert L. (Bert) Lasher, ca. 1928, owner of Musa Isle Seminole Indian Village (1922–32), Osceola Gardens Indian Village (1933–35), and Osceola's Indian Village (1937–43), provided the *i:laponathli:* leadership with publicity, a forum, and advice while operating the most famous tourist attractions in Miami. By permission of the Seminole/Miccosukee Photographic Archive, Fort Lauderdale, no. 835.

SEMINOLES! The Only American Indians Whom Your Uncle
Sam Never Conquered or Ruled.

Above: 9. Rotogravure
photograph, February 26,
1937. The caption pro-
motes the Seminoles'
"unconquered" status. By
permission of the Semi-
nole/Miccosukee Photo-
graphic Archive, Fort
Lauderdale, no. 1297.

Right: 10. Alan W. Davis,
lecturer, ca. 1928, then
foreman of Musa Isle
Seminole Indian Village,
1922–32, posing with
Josie Billie (Panther
Clan), a prominent doc-
tor and member of the
traditional *i:laponathli:*
council. By permission of
the Seminole/Miccosukee
Photographic Archive,
Fort Lauderdale, no. 646.

11. Musa Isle alligator wrestler Henry Sam Willie (né Henry Nelson) performs one of the most dangerous stunts, 1937. Photograph by Florence I. Randle, WPA. By permission of the Seminole/Miccosukee Photographic Archive, Fort Lauderdale, no. 222.

12. The wedding of Musa Isle headman Tony Tommie (Panther Clan) and Edna Johns (Big Towns) at Musa Isle Seminole Indian Village, June 4, 1926. As the village filled to capacity, spectators climbed into the *chickee* thatch for a view of the ceremony. Gleason Waite Romer, photographer. By permission of the Miami-Dade Public Library System, Romer Collection, no. 9c.

Above: 13. Palmetto-thatched pylons at the entrance to the Seminole Village attraction at the Canadian National Exhibition, Toronto, August 1931. Barkers announced the alligator wrestling shows which drew capacity crowds. All of the cypress wood for the Village *chickees*, palmetto fans for thatch, and coconut trees for landscaping were packed into boxcars and shipped to Canada from Miami. By permission of the Seminole/Miccosukee Photographic Archive, Fort Lauderdale, no. 178.

Left: 14. Cory R. Osceola (Big Towns Clan), February 15, 1927. He was headman for the Musa Isle Seminole Indian Village, 1926–30. Called "Chief" by the media, he became the spokesman for the traditional *i:laponathli:* council and assisted their lawyer, O. B. White. He was later the leader of the Independent Seminoles in Collier County. Claude C. Matlack, photographer. By permission of the National Anthropological Archives, Smithsonian Institution, no. 1178g.

Above: 15. Children pose with the popular alligator prop at Musa Isle Seminole Indian Village, ca. 1932. *Left to right, back row:* unidentified, unidentified, Douglas Osceola, Tommy Tiger, Mike Osceola, Homer Osceola, Buffalo Tiger, Bobby Tiger; *front row:* Howard Osceola, unidentified, Mary Jim Osceola, Lois Tiger Billie, Annie Tiger Jim, Agnes Osceola Cypress, Peggy Jim Osceola. Children often received 25 cents for posing. By permission of the Seminole/Miccosukee Photographic Archive, Fort Lauderdale, no. 883.

Left: 16. *I:laponathli:* woman sewing patchwork clothing on a treadle sewing machine at Musa Isle Seminole Indian Village, ca. 1920. Frank A. Robinson, photographer. By permission of the Seminole/Miccosukee Photographic Archive, Fort Lauderdale, no. 50.

17. Sightseeing boats brought a large daily percentage of tourists to the waterfront attractions of Coppinger's Tropical Gardens and Musa Isle. Tourists from the *Dixie*, which served Coppinger's attraction, pose for the photo concessioner, December 5, 1934. By permission of the Seminole/Miccosukee Photographic Archive, Fort Lauderdale, no. 1630.

18. Musa Isle was serviced by the *Seminole Queen* sightseeing boat, seen docking at its berth at Pier 6, Biscayne Bay, March 12, 1942. By permission of the Seminole/Miccosukee Photographic Archive, Fort Lauderdale, no. 97.3.16.

Left: 19. Buffalo Tiger (Bird Clan), a young artist at Musa Isle Seminole Indian Village, mid-1930s. He would be elected the first chairman of the Miccosukee Tribe of Indians of Florida in 1961. Bureau of Indian Affairs. Photograph by permission of the National Archives, no.75-N-SEM-16.

Below: 20. Tourist Dr. Irene Austin poses with two *i:laponathli:* children on the alligator prop at the Musa Isle photo concession, March 26, 1935. By permission of the Seminole/Miccosukee Photographic Archive, Fort Lauderdale, no. 94.38.1.

21. Mrs. John Tiger cuts up a roasted gar fish on a palmetto fan while Mickey Tiger (Bird Clan) cooks on the camp fire at Musa Isle, ca. 1937. Florence I. Randle, WPA, photographer. By permission of the Seminole/Miccosukee Photographic Archive, Fort Lauderdale, no. 243.

22. The family of Mrs. Lee Billie Cypress (Panther Clan) lived seasonally at the Silver Springs Seminole Village, Ocala, where her husband, Charlie Cypress (Otter Clan), was headman of the village. February 4, 1939. Burgert Bros. Photographic Studio, Tampa. By permission of the Seminole/Miccosukee Photographic Archive, Fort Lauderdale, no. 91.5P.12.

23. A group of 64 *i:laponathli:* was escorted by W. Stanley Hanson, Sr., to an engagement at the Bok Singing Tower attraction in Lake Wales, ca. 1937. They pose with Bok Tower officials and Hanson (in a Seminole jacket) *(standing far right)*. By permission of the Seminole/Miccosukee Photographic Archive, Fort Lauderdale, no. 88.5.7A.

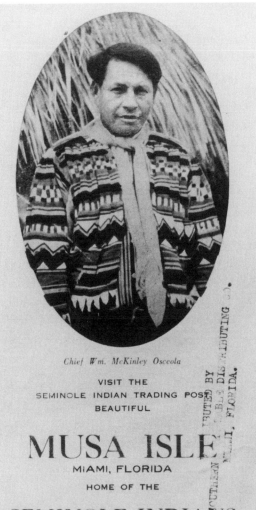

Chief *Wm. McKinley Osceola*

VISIT THE
SEMINOLE INDIAN TRADING POST
BEAUTIFUL

MUSA ISLE

MIAMI, FLORIDA

HOME OF THE

SEMINOLE INDIANS

ALLIGATOR AND CROCDILE FARM
MUSEUM AND ZOO OF FLORIDA SWAMP LIFE

Wm. Osceola, a direct descendant of the famous old chieftain, Robert Osceola, will be seen here as Chief of the present tribe. Robert Osceola was the old Chief who spent his life and finally died that his tribesmen might receive justice.

A SHOWPLACE FOR OVER 28 YEARS

24. Musa Isle brochure with a cover photo of William McKinley Osceola (Big Towns), headman of Bert Lasher's Indian villages, 1930–43. Photos by Florence I. Randle, WPA. By permission of the Seminole/Miccosukee Photographic Archive, Fort Lauderdale, no. 96.3.1.

25. At the beginning of a new tourist season the Seminole villages received a facelift. The sign for Osceola's Indian Village, operated by Bert Lasher in 1937–43, is being re-painted. By permission of the Seminole/Miccosukee Photographic Archive, Fort Lauderdale, no. 91.5P.7.

26. The early tourist attraction of Effie (Wind Clan) and Ingraham Billie's (Panther Clan) on the Tamiami Trail, 1938. Ingraham was a traditional councilman, doctor, and major medicine bundle carrier for the *i:laponathli:*. Their attraction was among one of the earliest Indian-owned and -operated tourist attractions on the Trail. By permission of the Seminole/Miccosukee Photographic Archive, Fort Lauderdale, no. 64.

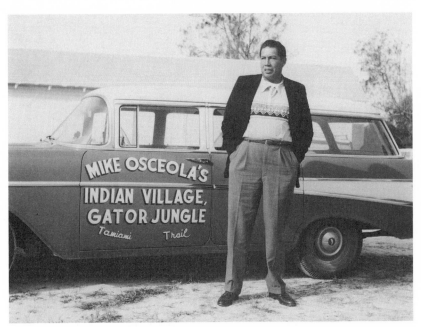

27. Larry Mike Osceola (Bird Clan) at his tourist attraction village on the Tamiami Trail, 1950s. Russell I. Peithman, photographer. By permission of the Florida State Archives, no. 83-025-240.

28. Joe Jimmie (Bird Clan), alligator wrestler at Tropical Paradise (site of Coppinger's), ca. 1965. By permission of the Seminole/Miccosukee Photographic Archive, Fort Lauderdale, no. 996.

29. Okalee Indian Village and Seminole Arts and Crafts building, Hollywood Seminole Indian Reservation, 1959. By permission of the Seminole/Miccosukee Photographic Archive, Fort Lauderdale, no. 95.78.1.

30. Hollywood Hard Rock Hotel and Casino, on the former site of Seminole Okalee Indian Village, Hollywood, Florida. 2007. By permission of the Seminole/Miccosukee Photographic Archive, Fort Lauderdale, no. 2007.2.5.

CHAPTER 10

"Off-Season" Economics

These Trail Indians are beginning to have an identity of their own.
Ethel Cutler Freeman, 1939b

In 1915, dredges had begun to dig up soil for the roadbed of the highway which would cross 110 miles of the Everglades, connecting Miami with the west coast city of Tampa. The construction of the Tamiami Trail was a huge undertaking funded by small, inadequate bond issues. As impatience grew over the lack of progress, twenty-three businessmen from both coasts, calling themselves "Trail Blazers," gathered a convoy of eleven vehicles at Fort Myers. On April 4, 1923, the entourage began a journey across fifteen miles of the watery, uncompleted expanse of the Tamiami Trail toward Miami. Guiding the travelers between Collier and Dade counties were *i:laponathli:* Little Billie (Wind, Josie and Ingraham Billie's father) and Abraham Lincoln Clay (Panther). It was estimated at the time that this unique and arduous publicity stunt resulted in 25,000 columns of front page publicity across the nation (*American Eagle* 1937). Interest in the project was rekindled, and the Tamiami Trail was completed as U.S. Highway 41, opening five years later on April 25, 1928.

As the marl roadway began to rise above the shallow inland sea of the River of Grass, the *i:laponathli:* watched as yet another portion of their environment was altered by machine-age progress. The completed Trail greatly impacted them as it cut directly across their canoe trails and impeded their travel. Sturtevant noted from discussions with Josie Billie in the 1950s, "Many locations near the Tamiami Trail are still oriented in his mind in relation to the now-obliterated Everglades canoe trails, rather than the highway" (1955:42).

But the Trail did what nothing else could have done for *i:laponathli:* economy. As soon as construction began on the roadbed, they made use of it as a handy place to camp above the water en route to and from Miami. Near the city, tour buses added the Indians' temporary camps to their sightseeing route, and photographs documented Seminoles canoeing down the Trail's barrow pit, the Tamiami Canal (Matlack 1921; Coppinger 1975). Once the highway opened, a steady stream of auto traffic brought the tourists into the *i:laponathli:'* environs and compelled the *i:laponathli:* to move from their isolated camps "out to the road." In 1936, W. Stanley Hanson noted:

> At the present time, there are a number of Seminoles who have acquired the ways and language of the white man to such an extent that they are able to conduct their own stores and their own amusement camps along the Tamiami Trail. Among these Seminoles there are William McKinley Osceola, Josie Billie, Chestnut Billie, Corey Osceola, Johnny Osceola, Ingram Billie, and Robert Billie.
>
> Mac [usually called Mike] Osceola, 17 year old son of William McKinley Osceola, who speaks excellent English, has developed the art of sign painting to such an extent that he paints all the signs used on the Tamiami Trail which advertise his father's Indian amusement village, situated 30 miles west of Miami.

D. Graham Copeland, an official of Collier County, through which the trail passed on its way to Tampa, related information to Ethel Cutler Freeman in 1939 concerning the Trail Indian camps. He stated "that 1/3 of the Indians in Collier County have come out [of the Big Cypress] and camped on the Trail and that though some called them commercialized, they were still so crude and simple that he didn't think their ways had changed much" (Freeman 1939a). Freeman visited the area herself later that year and made these observations:

It is only within the last two years that many Indians have made it [the Trail] their headquarters. This year there are thirteen camps. [They] sell what they make to tourists and charge sightseers admission to their villages. These villages are not temporary abodes or show places, but are their real homes during certain seasons. Although the Indians have left their homes in the wilds to gain a living from tourists, these camps along the Trail are not commercialized as one would expect. They live their lives independent of the white man who comes to look at them.

In this way they are comparable with the owners of the old houses of Virginia and England who open their homes and gardens for gain—yet they are not seen and their lives are untouched and unaffected by their visitors to whom they are supremely indifferent. (1939b)

The Trail villages were typically surrounded by an eight-foot fence of palmetto fronds. One entered through a *chickee* where an attendant sat to take the entrance fee. A modest selection of crafts and clothing for sale was arranged on tables or racks. According to Freeman, the village area was usually empty, the children and others having fled at the stranger's approach. An older woman remained sitting on the work platform sewing. The thatched, high-roofed cooking *chickee* was always found in the center of the village, usually with a clump of bananas at one side and with a small garden of sugarcane, corn, pumpkins, and sweet potatoes. Chickens, pigs, and dogs ran about. Sometimes an alligator or some other Everglades animal was penned. A hand pump was sunk into a shallow well for the camp's use (ibid.).

These camps operated by the *i:laponathli:* are important: they mark an increased economic independence for these Native Americans separate from the white-operated attractions in the city. They had apprenticed in the development of an economy and now established permanent, tangible bases from which to maintain their life-style and maintain their freedom from the government.

W. Stanley Hanson and R. Carl Liddle compiled data on the Trail villages in September 1936 for Ethel Cutler Freeman under the title "Seminole (Commercial) Camps on Tamiami Trail Going from Fort Myers to Miami":

Robert Billy's Camp: on left at Fickahatchee Station. Robert Billie, head man. From five to fifteen Indians. Indian curios for sale at store. Small zoo in connection with store—alligators, coons, turtles, on exhibit. Excellent English spoken by Robert Billy. Admission 15 [cents].

Ingram Billy's Camp: on right at Turner's River. Ingram Billy, head man. From ten to twenty Indians. Store. Neat camp built on old prehistoric Indian mound. Fair English spoken. Old "Doctor Tiger" a most picturesque Indian of the old days conducts store. Admission 15 [cents].

Josie Billy's Camp. On right, two miles beyond Ingram Billy's camp. Josie Billy, head man. Store. Florida animals, collection of orchids. Excellent English spoken by Josie Billy. A neat, new camp erected, 1936. Ten to fifteen Indians. Admission 15 [cents].

Johnny Osceola's camp. On left at Monroe Station. Johnny Osceola, head man. From fifteen to twenty-five Indians. Store. Florida animals on exhibit. Large, interesting camp. Excellent English spoken. Admission 15 [cents].

Corey Osceola's Camp. On right. One of the largest of the Indian stores, well filled with Seminole goods. Usual assortment of Florida animals. Corey Osceola, head man. Excellent English spoken. From five to twelve Indians. Admission 15 [cents].

Chestnut Billy's Camp. On left at Paolita Station. A large camp. Store. Usual zoo of Florida animals. From fifteen to twenty-five Indians. Excellent English spoken. Chestnut Billy, head man. Admission 15 [cents].

John Motlo's Camp. On right, just past Collier County stone arch. John Motlo, head man. Usual zoo of Florida animals. From five to ten Indians. Store. Good English spoken. Admission 15 [cents].

William McKinley Osceola's Camp. On right, about ten miles towards Miami from State "Y" camp. In Everglades proper. From fifteen to twenty-five Indians. William McKinley Osceola, head man. Large camp. Large store. Seminole goods and curios. McKinley and his sons all speak excellent English. This camp has possibly the largest and best kept zoo of Florida animals. Crocodiles to be seen. A general store is maintained here by the Seminole owner. Groceries for sale to tourists.

Musa Isle foreman Alan Davis described the economics of the Trail camps: "It didn't cost anything much to live there. . . . If you got enough money to buy flour and rice and canned tomatoes and corn, corn meal, he'd have all the fish and meat that he wanted" (Davis 1980). It would seem that these tourist attractions were capable, then, of turning a profit for the *i:laponathli:* entrepreneurs.

The Tamiami Trail and its new assemblage of Indian camps were news. A clipping from *Hartford* (Connecticut) *Courant* of February 1937 had the headline "Tamiami Trail in Florida Leads to Indian Villages" and this story:

> From Miami the seven million dollar highway presents variations in the habits of the tribes. Not far from the resort are the fixed habitation trading centers of the Seminole merchants who offer from their reed and grass thatched emporiums Indian products of hand-made miniature canoes, baskets, dolls, and beads. Beyond the Preserve are the itinerant peddlers who offer deer hides and antlers and skins for rugs, while deeper into the Everglades are the more primitive settlements, with their huts and cypress dug-out canoe.
>
> "To reach the Seminoles along the new trail which extends East and West, there are a number of settlements within easy accessibility of resort trains," states C. E. Bell, passenger Traffic Manager of the Seaboard Air Line Railway, who cites how there are convenient highways to the villages from the routes of both the East and West Coast "Orange Blossom Specials." Since the opening of the trail and the rail facilities, visits to the native Seminole haunts are becoming a fascinating tourist diversion.

Reporters sometimes took another stance in their reporting of *i:laponathli:* entrepreneurship. A headline of 1938 in *Resorts* read, "Seminoles by the Road: Along the Tamiami Trail in Florida They Lie in Wait to Welcome the Tourists. There they lure the passing traveler like any concessionaire along Atlantic City's boardwalk." Another read, "Now the more civilized tribes live in camps along the Tamiami Trail and make a surprisingly good living by shaking down boggle-eyed tourists" (*Courier-Journal* n.d.).

The Trail was known for something other than its Indian population. It had beome a dangerous roadway. The *Chicago Tribune* (1933) wrote about "motorists who speed over the Trail and catch a glimpse of some of the colorfully dressed Indians along the highway." The *Ft. Myers News Press* (1937a) alarmed the state with the headline "Trail Deaths Mount; State Aroused." Accidents sometimes occurred because of the colorful Indians living along the roadway: "Mr. and Mrs. O. E. Ayers of Filson, Illinois, and their son were en route to Miami when the boy spied a Seminole camp beside the trail. He leaned over from the back seat to attract his father's attention and Mr. Ayers lost control of the car, swung his Plymouth sedan into an approaching Cadillac and then caromed into the canal" (*Ft. Myers News Press* 1935). While these fortunate tourists lived, numbers of tourists and a number of *i:laponathli:* lost their lives along this roadway and in the Tamiami Canal.

Infrequent gas stations became important landmarks between Naples and Miami. Weaver's Station was one of these. Robert and Suzie Billie moved there from their camp in Big Cypress around 1938 to capitalize on the tourist traffic (Billie 1990).

The *i:laponathli:* living in Seminole villages along the Tamiami Trail developed another opportunity, one consistent with their hunting traditions: The men were hired as hunting guides or contracted to procure game for clients. This business had good and bad repercussions. The *Ft. Myers News Press* was quoted in 1935 in the *Ft. Pierce News Tribune* saying that the Seminoles had "killed off all of the game and sold it to Miami butcher shops" (1935). Wild turkeys were selling from $2.50 to $3.00 and a deer at $12.00 "f.o.b. Tamiami Trail." This article inferred that the Seminoles had killed off all the game yet contradicted itself by saying that if a hunter did not wish to return home empty-handed, he could buy game from a Seminole hunter on the Trail. "The Indians are permitted to hunt the year around without a license and can't be pinched for having game in their possession but they have heard there is such a thing as a game warden and that it is bad medicine to sell one of them meat. So they trade only through channels with which they are acquainted, there apparently being plenty of same."

Government investigator Roy Nash had noted the illegal trafficking in game by the *i:laponathli:* in 1930, when venison brought the hunter around fifty cents a pound: "A car speeds along the Tamiami Trail and pulls up beside an Indian. 'John, I go Ft. Myers, come back 4 o'clock. Pennawaw , [Creek for turkey] $2?' On his way back to Miami, the white man receives a wild turkey and the Indian his $2. Also an illegal transaction." (1931:37). Answering an inquiry made by Nash on this subject, the state game commissioner replied that they were planning to "use every effort to stop" the Indians from selling game. "We feel that the Indians should be placed in a reservation and be required to stay there and allowed to hunt in this reservation for their own use, but not for the market" (Nash 1931:37, 43).

However, by 1937, an emergency arose, causing the Seminole Indian Association to call a special meeting. The *i:laponathli:* were being "pushed near the brink of starvation by white vandalage upon their almost sole subsistence of game, furs, fish, and alligator skins—the game, their main meat; the furs and skins, their money crop" (*Lake Wales Daily* 1937). The association suggested that the whites be "shut off from all hunting and trapping in all and every region . . . of home and hunting grounds of all the Seminoles, and reserving to them the Tamiami Trail frontage privileges on both sides for sale of their handiwork and for the incidental cultural contact with the whites." In 1937 the hunting season for deer was "November 20 to December 31; turkey from November 20 to February 15; and doves and quail from November 20 to February 15. Panther, bear and wildcats may be hunted any time. State hunting licenses cost $25 for tourists and $8 for residents of the state. Seminole Indians may be obtained as guides and with a brave in charge of the expedition the hunter rarely fails to fill his bag" (*Ft. Myers News Press* 1937c).

Meanwhile, as it became increasingly apparent that the Florida Seminole could use some aid, there continued to be few Indian residents on the Hollywood Reservation. The isolated Big Cypress Reservation in Hendry County, closed since 1926, was reopened. Around forty miles southeast of Fort Myers, this reservation is important to a study of the Tamiami Trail camps and tourism in general. The *i:laponathli:* inhabitants of this region were involved in the Miami attractions and many had villages on the Trail. These people had also been taken by Hanson to the Dade Battle commemoration in 1936 and to Bok Tower in 1936–37 to earn tourist attraction income. During significant periods in the 1930s they moved from the Trail to the reservation and back again. In time, many of these former antigovernment *i:laponathli:* would become permanent residents of the Big Cypress Reservation.

In a stroke of genius, Special Commissioner Francis J. Scott hired Hanson to oversee the Big Cypress programs as caretaker of the Hendry County (Big Cypress) Reservation. Hanson, of course, was far more knowledgeable of the *i:laponathli:*' needs than the federal agents, so he would finally have a chance to accomplish what he had sought for so long. He would not have the title of Seminole agent, but he would finally be working with the *i:laponathli:* in an official capacity.

There were nine adults and five children on the reservation land when Hanson arrived in 1937. In the next year, ninety persons would arrive. Freeman (1938) gave full credit to Hanson. Like the agents, Hanson had come to be concerned that for the long term, the *i:laponathli:* would require a reservation, with perhaps a more stable income than that from seasonal tourism and crop picking. However, conceding to live on the reservation brought economic and religious/political changes that would in time be the turning point for the majority of *i:laponathli:*.

Scott was anxious for Hanson to introduce new economic opportunities for his new reservation residents. In actuality these benefits had been included in the government concessions, spinoffs from Commissioner Collier's meeting with the *ci:saponathli:* in 1935. Among the New Deal improvements for Big Cypress were a cattle program, roads, bridges, fencing, pasture improvement, and general upgrading of buildings and communication services for the new economic development, all built with Indian labor for which the community received the improvements and the individuals their pay under the Civilian Conservation Corps–Indian Division. Hanson found it difficult to persuade *i:laponathli:* workers that it was alright to sign for their wages because, after all, it was government money. He was persuasive and persistent, and gradually the CCC-ID program became stable, winning plaudits from none other than Collier himself (West 1994).

However, it was this program, along with conversions to Christianity, that would break down the traditional leadership, creating a greater division between the reservation dwellers and the slowly dwindling number of antigovernment *i:laponathli:*. The cattle program required men to act in nontraditional leadership roles, to head up committees, to make decisions. Often decisions were made by individuals who in the traditional system might not belong to a leadership clan or have enough political stature to make them (King 1978:90–104). Thus it was the economic freedom of tourism that had allowed the nonreservation *i:laponathli:* to preserve their polity.

But in the last days of 1939 another crisis loomed that appeared to affect the livelihood of the *i:laponathli:*. In a continuing effort to quell an outbreak of "deer tick fever" which killed cattle, a general slaughter of deer had been systematically carried out across the United States. In Florida, the deer had been eradicated in all but two counties, Hendry and Collier. Agent Scott learned that the State of Florida wanted permission to kill all of the deer on the Hendry County Reservation. Under the auspices of spokesman Cory Osceola, the *i:laponathli:* protested loudly, sending a telegram directly to Secretary of the Interior Harold Ickes. Ickes sent Commissioner John Collier to meet with the Seminoles. The *i:laponathli:* representatives at this historic meeting were Cory Osceola (Big Towns), William McKinley Osceola (Big Towns), Frank Tiger (Bird), Cuffney Tiger (Otter), John Osceola (Big Towns), Josie Billie (Panther), John Cypress (Panther), and James Truitt Osceola (Big Towns). They were joined by three *ci:saponathli:*, John Josh (Deer), Willie Gopher, Sr. (Bird), and Richard Osceola (Bird), officers of the Seminole Cattlemen's Association at Brighton Reservation, who made the long trip to meet with Collier at Bayfront Park in Miami (*Miami News* 1940).

The Seminole were firm that the deer must be preserved. Collier's suggestion was to kill the deer, then have the reservation restocked with tick-free deer in two years. But when Ickes and Collier had visited in 1934, they had promised to "protect forever the reservation and their wild life" (*Newsweek* 1942:33). Upon meeting resistance to any adverse plans, Collier decided not to make enemies and ordered a "deeper study" of the disease. This postponed the slaughter date. Results from the new study showed that the initial study by the Department of Agriculture was not conclusive enough to order the destruction of deer as the sole carriers of the disease (Philip 1977:33). The reservation deer herds were thus saved.

In this watchdog manner, Cory Osceola and the *i:laponathli:* councilmen continued to act for *i:laponathli:* rights at large, even though some of their number had become reservation residents. It was typical that these leaders did not choose to deal with local Seminole Agency officials but went over their heads to Washington, to communicate with their acquaintances Harold Ickes and John Collier.

Secretary Ickes' ruling to spare the deer on the Seminole Reservation was strongly opposed by Governor Fred P. Cone, who represented the interests of the Florida Cattlemen's Association. Cone stated in a telegram to Ickes, "It is foolish to wreck a $20,000,000 industry just to protect a few ticky deer" (*Miami Herald* 1940).

To appease the Department of Agriculture under Senator Claude Pepper and to keep the Indians' deer contained on reservation property, Ickes had a seven-foot-high fence constructed around the reservation. The important decision to protect the *i:laponathli:'* traditional food supply cost the federal government $75,000 for periodic dipping of cattle near the reservation, several thousand dollars for research, and $40,000 for the fence (*Newsweek* 1942:33).

Draft registration prior to U.S. involvement in World War II created yet another crisis for the *i:laponathli:*. They refused to register for the draft, not so much because they would not fight for the land but because they adamantly opposed signing their names or making their mark on the forms (see King 1978:21). In this they were supported by the *i:laponathli:* council. The CCC-ID program could not pay the workers if they did not sign their draft cards, which caused hardships and additional distrust. Mothers hid their grown sons and sons-in-law, then fled the Big Cypress

Reservation to go into isolation in the wilds of the Big Cypress. Camps on the Tamiami Trail were enlarged to accommodate families who fled the reservation.

The Miami tourist attractions also became havens for refugees from the reservation. Cory Osceola, Josie Billie, John Osceola, William Mc-Kinley Osceola, as well as Bert Lasher and even W. Stanley Hanson (who was to register the Seminoles), were labeled "recalcitrants" by Seminole agent Dwight Gardin. He went so far as to turn in their names to the Federal Bureau of Investigation for inciting the Indians against the draft registration, but that agency had more pressing matters to prosecute (West 1993).

Additional economic subsistence for the *i:laponathli:* on the Trail was seasonal crop picking (see Kersey 1986). This type of work became more important as members of south Florida's general workforce enlisted or were drafted during World War II. It was by way of this important employment that many of the antiregistration *i:laponathli:* families, including those of Cory and William McKinley Osceola, actually contributed to the war effort under such headlines as "Seminoles Aid War Effort," "Doing Their Bit to Win the War," "The Seminoles Have Gone to War . . . fighting the battle of production" (West 1993:17).

By the early 1940s the Trail *i:laponathli:* had begun to develop an economy based on frog meat. Finding their boats too slow, the mechanically astute *i:laponathli:* followed the lead of inventive white frog hunters and made their own "airboat," one driven by an airplane propeller, for night hunting in the Everglades (Hanson 1944). *I:laponi:* Willie Frank (Wind), one of the first to make a new airboat, told Hanson that in six nights he gigged $150 worth of frogs. Long after the flush of this brief but lucrative economy waned because of the emergence of cheaper Japanese suppliers, the popular airboats are still used by *i:laponathli:* men as unique vehicles to take tourists around their Everglades environs.

The Tamiami Trail villages became viable business locations and focal areas for many nonreservation *i:laponathli:* families. Sturtevant observed, "One result of the Tamiami Trail has been a realignment and overlapping of groups that were previously geographically more distinct. The region toward the town of Everglades at the south end of the Big Cypress Swamp began to be occupied by families from the northern Big Cypress about 1882. Later, these moved north to the Trail, while others who had remained in the Big Cypress moved south to the highway, both meeting those who had moved west from the Miami–Fort Lauderdale region" (1971:115).

Most of the Trail villages continued to be used as off-season abodes for families who had not made a complete break from the city attractions. For others, such as Cory Osceola, the Trail camp was the family's permanent place of residence, and they left it only to engage in seasonal crop picking. Cory Osceola continued to officiate as the political spokesman for the Trail camp and, with encouragement from his longtime friend Alan W. Davis, was one of the first *i:laponathli:* actually to purchase land on which to build their attraction village in the 1950s. Councilman Ingraham Billie could also be reached at a Trail village that had become a strategic location for persons who were responsible for the affairs of the *i:laponathli:*. It was no casual observation when Ethel Cutler Freeman commented, "These Trail Indians are beginning to have an identity of their own" (1939b).

CHAPTER 11

The Opposition

Exhibit arts and crafts, but not people.

Deaconess Harriet M. Bedell

In *The White Man's Indian*, Robert F. Berkhofer, Jr., discusses the concept of the "good" Indian and the "bad" Indian throughout history, noting, "Indians lacked certain or all aspects of white civilization [and] could be viewed as bad or good depending upon the observer's feelings about his own society and the use to which he wanted to put the image. In line with this possibility, commentators upon the history of white imagery of the Indian have found two fundamental but contradictory conceptions of Indian culture" (1978:27–28).

This phenomenon can be seen in south Florida. In the late nineteenth and early twentieth century, before the Everglades were drained, the *i:laponathli:'* life-style was generally applauded by settlers and scientists alike (MacCauley 1887; Cory 1896). But once the alterations in their environment created economic changes and the *i:laponathli:* were employed in the fledgling tourist attraction business, a change in attitude toward them could be noted. They no longer seemed the "Lords of Nature" or "Nimrod" figures, images they had previously personified. It was then assumed that they had been "exploited" and were exhibited like "monkeys and alligators" in the tourist attractions. The attractions were themselves considered "great sore spots" in the Indians' lives. The *i:laponathli:* employed by the tourist attractions were "the poorest type" and "lazy outcasts" (Stirling 1936:9; *Miami Herald* [quoting Bedell] 1937; Freeman 1939b; Florida Writers' Project [quoting Gardin] 1941:38).

Early in the twentieth century a series of studies had been made on the Florida Seminoles. The first was a report from government investigator Samuel A. Eliot (1919), and he set the tone for future negative commentaries about the nonreservation "Seminoles" who earned "exhibition" income. Just two years after the *i:laponathli:* had begun their formal relationship with tourism, he wrote, "There are two or three Indian camps adjacent to the winter resorts, but these people evidently go to the neighborhood of Miami or Ft. Lauderdale largely for show purposes and *do not represent the condition and spirit of the tribe*" (italics mine).

The *i:laponathli:'* tourist attraction economy escalated. In 1930, thirteen years into it, Clement C. Ucker of the Board of the United States Indian Commissioners wrote a *Report on the Seminole Indians of Florida*, which was published in its entirety in the *Miami Daily News* (1930a). Ucker stated that the "Seminoles" had been "piteously exploited," that there were "alarming social and moral conditions . . . due directly to 'bootleg' liquor and the harboring of girls in so-called 'places of amusement' back of Miami."

Based on Ucker's findings, Charles J. Rhodes, head of the Bureau of Indian Affairs from 1929 to 1933, compiled and submitted his recommendations as requested by President Herbert J. Hoover. Reported in the *Ft. Myers News Press* (1930), the Bureau of Indian Affairs planned to save "the red man's self-respect from the ravages of an exhibitionist age." More formally stated, "It is the purpose of the Bureau of Indian Affairs to discourage the proclivity of the average Indian to participate in circuses, rodeos, wild west shows and similar enterprises and in lieu thereof to direct him to a more permanent dignified means of livelihood" (*Ocala Morning Banner* 1930). In the official document, Ucker (1930) had proposed "an Act for the preservation and protection of the Seminole Indian of Florida." Among other things, it would make it "a misdemeanor under state law to harbor these Indians for amusement purposes."

Tony Tommie had been temporarily cured of tuberculosis by 1930. According to the *Miami Daily News* (1930b), upon his release from a sanitorium in Shawnee, Oklahoma, he had been taken on a tour through Oklahoma, Arizona, New Mexico, and California as a goodwill representative of the government. Tommie returned to Miami just as Ucker's report hit the press. Interestingly, he arrived just in time to serve as the supposedly credible native spokesperson whose insider knowledge supported the government investigator's findings "that the Seminoles are being weakened physically and morally, through the oppression of vicious whites" (*Palm Beach Post* 1930).

But Cory Osceola had replaced Tommie as the headman and media liaison of Musa Isle Village and had taken on the responsibility of caring for the inhabitants of the Miami village. He found himself taking Ucker's accusations personally. The *Palm Beach Post* (1930) reported, "[Cory Osceola, who] described himself as 'boss' of the East Coast Indians since Tommy's departure, denied the charges generally. He asserted that they were exaggerated and that the health conditions of the Indians under him are excellent, with a few exceptions."

Ucker died shortly after completing his report, but his work and his views were liberally championed by Special Agent Roy Nash (1931) in his *Survey of the Seminole Indians of Florida*, published as Senate Document Number 314 (1931). Nash's study contains valuable data on the Seminoles, but the work was biased against the tourist attractions and "certain" Indians who found employment with them: "To the commercial villages in Miami, St. Petersburg, and others which may spring up, I would grant no quarter. These places point the road to stagnation and death.... Earning one's living in competition with rattlesnakes and alligators leads nowhere" (39, 81).

During the 1930 tourist season, the Blind Pass Seminole village had opened in St. Petersburg and became part of Nash's 1930 tourist attraction employment statistics. This was a novel attraction located on Treasure Island at Blind Pass. It could only be reached by boat from the terminus of the St. Petersburg streetcar line. It was short lived, operating for only two seasons, but its presence in a city outside of Miami became a significant statistic in Roy Nash's survey (West 1986a). His recommendation, based on the opening of the St. Pete attraction, was that "inasmuch as the obnoxious commercial villages have been organized in more than one Florida city, the Florida legislature should be asked for a law 'making it a misdemeanor to harbor these Indians for amusement purposes'" (Nash 1931:85–86).

Perhaps the most disturbing evidence brought to light by Nash's official reports came from two government contract physicians, one in Miami and the other in Fort Myers. These doctors who administered to the *i:laponathli:* in their jurisdictions claimed that, of the few cases of social disease among the *i:laponathli:*, all of them could be traced back to Musa Isle and Coppinger's Pirate's Cove. In his zeal to close the attractions, Nash wrote to Miami's mayor C. H. Reeder on November 1, 1930, suggesting that on the basis of this information, "It would be a splendid thing if the City of Miami would prohibit Indian Villages within her borders." However, the Miami city commissioners "were under the opinion that the camps were assets to the city and beneficial to the Indians because they provided them with trading posts for the furs and skins they obtained in the Everglades" (*Miami Herald* 1930; Nash 1931:44, 45).

City Commissioner E. G. Sewell proclaimed the Musa Isle camp "historical" as well as "an attraction for winter visitors." Martha Lasher and Cory Osceola of Musa Isle protested Nash's accusations before the Miami City Commission, as Osceola had previously protested those of Ucker (*Miami Herald* 1930). Musa Isle foreman Alan Davis (1980), when asked for his reaction to Nash's survey, replied, "Well, I felt just like the Seminoles did. It went in one ear and out the other. That was their way of life. I wasn't trying to change it. They didn't want to be changed and their camps in the 'Glades were the same way. We did keep Musa Isle more sanitary than the ones in the Glades."

Also affecting the wishes of government men who wanted to take charge of the *i:laponathli:'* lives was the ever-vigilant *i:laponathli:* council. As it grew more and more aware of their sovereign rights, it became a real threat to the agency's special commissioners James L. Glenn, Francis J. Scott, and Dwight Gardin. Between 1933 and 1941, *i:laponathli:* leaders dashed the commissioners' hopes and disrupted their plans, which in turn threatened their employment. Glenn's landmark meeting with New Deal officials was far less significant because of the *i:laponathli:* council's successful opposition efforts carried out by Cory Osceola, William McKinley Osceola, and attorney O. B. White. Gardin's authority suffered because of the council's opposition to *i:laponathli:* draft registration.

The lucrative economic advantages of the tourist attractions were not wasted on the residents of Dania Reservation. The craftswomen were not the only people who sought economic benefits in Miami. Agent Spencer had told a Senate Investigation Committee in 1930 that "the two amusement parks there are very detrimental to our work and we haven't enough money to prevent that. I pay an Indian $2.50 a day to work eight hours clearing land on the reservation. They pay him $2.50 a day to sit down and make a show of himself" (Kersey 1989:38). This intrusion disrupted the government reservation's scheduled work and the education programs.

But in fact, the reservation work program did not provide full-time employment. In the early 1930s, workloads were split up to give aid to as many workers as possible. The *ci:saponathli:* from the Dania Reservation periodically went to the Miami attractions to sell their crafts, then stayed on to earn salary. The reservation *ci:saponathli:* also earned off-season summer employment. "Regularly a truck was sent to the reservation at Dania [from Coppinger's] to take a load of Indians down for the day" (Nash 1931:81). But these people received government rations for living on the reservation. As a result Nash wrote, "I consider that the end justifies cutting off the rations of all Indians who accept this demoralizing employment."

The Indian Service paid for medical aid to the Seminole whether they lived on the reservation or not. That made the tourist attraction employees eligible for such care. In his hard line against the attractions, Nash also recommended "that the Government discontinue paying the doctor's bills for Indians making their living in commercial amusement camps" (ibid.).

Roy Nash had recommended the Reverend James L. Glenn for the position of special commissioner to the Florida Seminoles in 1930, and little wonder, as they shared the same strong views on tourist attraction employment. Glenn was selected over W. Stanley Hanson, the man who was the obvious choice of scores of important Floridians and the *i:laponathli:* themselves. Hanson had actually campaigned for the position and was heartily supported by politicians, newspaper editors, and prominent citizens who sent scores of letters and telegrams to the Indian Office in Washington (West 1994). But he was not selected. It was Hanson's insider knowledge, his genuine concern and support of the welfare of the *i:laponathli:*, perhaps also his past willingness to aid them in the pursuit of an exhibition income, that kept him from realizing his life's ambition. Glenn (and doubtless Nash) considered that the Seminole Indian Association, which Hanson had cofounded in 1913 and on whose board he served a lifetime position as secretary, was "a divisive influence which undercut governmental efforts to rehabilitate the tribe" (Kersey in Glenn 1982:58).

As an embittered special commissioner, Glenn expounded, in his prepared annual reports and his personal papers, on the undercutting of government efforts by the tourist attractions and their personnel. "The 'ballahoo' of these show places featured the Indians as an unconquered, unrelenting, and implacable enemy of the ways of the white man and especially of the white man's government. The management was represented as the great benefactor, and the government and its agent as the chief malefactors of the tribe." Further, he saw the attractions as "an effective blockade of the government's attempt to extend a program of justice and equity to their people" (U.S. Department of the Interior 1935:4). Glenn passionately described their plight: "To see the proud, and daring warrior reduced to the pit of the monkey, the bear, the snake, the alligator, and other strange and forgotten creatures of the earth is most pathetic, and assuredly is an injustice which the race, in its adjustment to the larger resources of more cultured people, ought never, never to be allowed to suffer" (U.S. Department of the Interior 1933:9).

Unfortunately, when Musa Isle foreman Alan Davis was interviewed at the Miami Depot as he escorted a group of *i:laponathli:* to the New York World's Fair in 1939, a reporter who covered the departure erroneously wrote in the *Miami Herald* (1939) that Davis was the U.S. Indian agent and that he was "chaperoning the party on the government's behalf." On his arrival in New York, Davis was confronted by Indian Service officials who interrogated him for two hours, took a lengthy deposition, and finally concluded that he was indeed innocent of misrepresentation (Davis 1981a).

In 1933, Nash and Glenn gained another fervent ally in their fight against the *i:laponathli:'* tourist attraction economy in Deaconess Harriet M. Bedell. She had begun her career in 1911 with the Cheyenne at Whirlwind Mission in northwestern Oklahoma. She then spent sixteen years with Alaskan natives at Steven's Village, just forty miles from the Arctic Circle. In semiretirement, she was invited to southeast Florida on a speaking engagement in Miami for the Florida Chain of Missionary Assemblies on January 21–26, 1933, while she waited for the diocese to appropriate funds for her work in retirement with the "Florida Seminoles." Bedell had also received an invitation from the Glenns, who were, according to her superior, the Bishop, Right Reverend John D. Wing (1933), "exceedingly anxious for you to come down to begin your work among the Indians."

While in Miami, she was taken to one of the Seminole Village tourist attractions. She confided in a reporter years later, "I went up to a group of men and held out my hand. I told them I had come to live among them and be their friend. They just glared and held their hands rigidly at their sides. I went over to the other side of the camp and put my hand on the shoulder of a woman. She shook it off coldly. I left there like a whipped puppy" (Smith 1959). While Bedell thought it was the *i:laponathli:'* exhibition lifestyle that was to blame for their aloofness, she did not realize that as a stranger, she had greatly overstepped the bounds of propriety.

Following the *i:laponathli:*' rebuke, Bedell left Miami to "state my opposition to these commercial villages to the state executive board meeting
of the Federation of Women's Clubs which was being held at Deland,
Florida" (Bedell 1933). The executive board of the Women's Clubs had
been familiar with the Seminoles' needs since the end of the nineteenth
century, mostly from the writings of Minnie Moore Willson and the more
recent welfare activities of board members Mrs. Frank (Ivy) Stranahan of
Fort Lauderdale, Mrs. Julia Hanson of Fort Myers (W. Stanley Hanson's
mother), and Mrs. Hicks Allen of Miami. But undoubtedly Deaconess
Bedell's fresh reaction of total indignation to the "Seminoles on exhibition" made a deep impression. Bedell would spend the remaining twenty-
seven years of her life in service to the *i:laponathli:*, hoping for Christian
conversions and attempting to wean them away from the tourist attractions by finding markets for the sale of their arts and crafts (West 1984).

Her next disappointment was that there were no funds in the church
budget to open her mission. Characteristic of this determined woman,
however, she took her pension and a monthly discretionary allowance of
$50 from the Executive Board of the Church Service League and contin-
ued her career with the Florida Seminoles at the reestablished Glade
Cross Mission at Everglades, Florida.

Like Glenn, Bedell's primary opposition to the tourist attractions was
that she found them "demeaning" to the Indians, feeling that the attractions were a barricade on the road to more appropriate economic opportunities. "Exhibit arts and crafts, but not people!" was the frequent admo-
nition she wrote in her newsletters and sternly said to reporters (Bedell
Papers).

Another in the long line of governmental studies on the Florida Seminoles was commissioned in 1936. The *Report on the Seminole Indians in
Florida* was undertaken by Gene Stirling from the Office of Indian Affairs'
new applied anthropology unit. In this brief study, Stirling made the following observations on life in the tourist attractions:

> The Miami exhibition camps are the great sore spots in the Semi-
> nole picture. The camps especially desire families with children.
> The Indians are given their food and a few dollars a week per family.
> They have nothing to do except to be looked at by the Tourists.
> Most of the cash they receive goes for liquor so that most of the
> nights are spent drinking. It is from these camps that most of the
> moral problems and venereal disease cases arise. They certainly offer
> a very unhealthy environment for the children to be brought up in.
> Two or three years of this loafing life with big city attractions makes
> the adults loath to take up a normal economic life again. The Semi-

noles are still too primitive to be in constant contact with a resort city like Miami without it doing them immeasurable harm. (1936:9)

In 1937 Bedell spoke at the Seminole Indian Association's annual meeting in Fort Myers. It was she who presented the opinion that the Indians were being exhibited "like monkeys and alligators" in the attractions of Miami (*Miami Herald* 1937).

Lecturers on Seminole welfare, such as Bedell, spoke frequently around the state, discussing openly their opposition to the *i:laponathli:'* tourist attraction economy. They continued to condemn the participants but failed to suggest a realistic alternative. The closest that they came to approving a related project was to suggest in 1936, when Everglades National Park was being proposed, that the Seminoles could have a role in this major project as guides and souvenir sellers—a novel idea indeed to the creators of this great federal project. Newspapers extolled the suggestion under the headline "Indians Get a Chance to Earn a Living!" (*Daytona Beach Independent* 1936).

The popular Florida Writers' Project publication *Seminole Indians in Florida*, published in 1941, served as the most serious work on the Seminole for many decades. It too included passages that attempted to sum up all the negative information associated with the Indians' tourist attraction experiences, however incidental. Unfortunately, it would wrongly influence generations of readers on the era of the "Seminoles on Exhibition." An example reads: "Commercial camps, operated by whites, are deplored by all who work sincerely for the benefit of the Seminole; the effect of liquor is degrading; the diseases of the white race have made their appearance among the Indians; there are some mixed-blood children and there is some immorality" (75).

Agent Dwight Gardin got a chance to vent his frustration against the attractions and their *i:laponathli:* employees in this same publication:

Life in the tourist centers, or in commercial camps owned and operated by white men, has not had a beneficial effect on the Seminole. During the past ten years, those so engaged have become more indolent, with a growing contempt for the white people who pay to see them.

The Indians engaged in the business of commercializing their race, are as a rule of the poorest type, often lazy outcasts and renegades from the tribe. They are looked upon with contempt by the higher type of Seminoles of the reservations and primitive camps who have little or no contact with tourists. (ibid.:38)

Gardin provided yet another example of the "good" and "bad" Indian in Florida: The "good" Indian lived on the reservation or in isolated "primitive" and unspoiled camps; the "bad" Indian was the one who earned his living in the city tourist attractions.

This viewpoint is all the more a smokescreen when data are gathered on incidences of intoxication and of violence, including sex crimes, that occurred outside the sphere of the city tourist attractions, in the Big Cypress, on the Tamiami Trail, and on the Dania Reservation itself. Agency personnel were most anxious to condemn incidents that could be pinpointed as originating from the attractions but were not interested in discussing the overall picture.

The Big Cypress was indeed an area of pristine native camps, but surrounding it was one of the last real frontiers. In this rough and tumble area, unscrupulous whites and blacks operated moonshine stills. There were documented incidents of intoxicated white men raping *i:laponathli:* women. More often, Indian men located the stills and helped themselves to the contents with sometimes fatal results. Intoxication and drunken brawls were commonplace, and some confrontations resulted in first- and second-degree murders that made all the state's papers.

One such case involved councilman and medicine man Josie Billie, who killed a woman in a drunken brawl on the Trail in 1928. He was taken by Hanson to the St. Petersburg (Blind Pass) tourist attraction to keep him safe from retaliation (Hanson n.d.; *St. Pete Independent* 1935; Glenn 1982:90, 110). Nor was the seat of the Seminole Agency spared. Agent Spencer wrote in 1927 that conditions regarding liquor on the reservation were "the worse that could be imagined." He stated grimly, "It drives the Indian crazy which has resulted in three deaths during the past year, two murders and one drowning" (Nash 1931:48). Thus it would seem that the commercial tourist attraction Indian villages were the scapegoat for all disruptive situations and disturbing conditions among the *i:laponathli:* over which government agents had no control.

It is unfortunate that the government did not make an attempt to review the Indians' involvement in the tourist attractions in a more realistic and workable light. However, they did not, and their idealistic plans for these Native Americans were in direct opposition to the job descriptions at the attractions and to the *i:laponathli:'* will. While the Hoover administration wanted to make the Indian "white," Roosevelt's man, John Collier, wanted them to remain tribal. While James L. Glenn, being a Hoover man, hated the attraction economy, Collier should have applauded them for their promotion of native ways. But the tourist attractions were seen in too negative a light for any positive effect on "tribalism" to come through.

The Meriam Report, a survey published in 1928, first addressed Native American arts and crafts as a viable reservation economy, but this view had not yet found its place in reservation policymaking in Florida (1928). The *ci:saponathli:* women at Dania Reservation had to travel over twenty miles to sell their wares at the Musa Isle Trading Post (Dade County Chancery Records 1932). There was no formal craft outlet on the reservation until 1938, when the federal government established one at the northernmost and newly created Brighton Reservation as part of Collier's New Deal concessions to the *ci:saponathli:*. The program was not expanded to include the Big Cypress *i:laponathli:* until 1953 (West 1996). It would have been a great economic advantage to these reservation women if a crafts outlet had been made available.

Had the government been supportive of the *i:laponathli:'* choice of economy, the Seminole Agency could have sponsored a tourist center and craft outlet in the 1930s as it did in the late 1950s. With such a program in place and with men and women coming to the reservation to sell their crafts, the opportunity would have made for better relations. The government then would not have appeared the hard-nosed protagonist, but such thoughts were inconceivable at the time.

There were few plaudits for the *i:laponathli:'* economic success in the tourist market. The press was the sole public champion. *The Miami Post* noted in 1930, "Indian villages such as Musa Isle and the Coppinger place, or those at Everglades help the Seminoles to make an honest dollar. And honest dollars are the only kind he knows how to make." The wizened ethnomusicologist Frances Densmore (1956) was sympathetic to Native American conditions as she visited reservations around the country recording their music. When visiting the Florida Seminoles in 1931, she applauded their economic efforts: "They have developed a commercial ability which makes them self-supporting, and they have succeeded in doing this with a minimum use of the English language."

By 1954, attorney O. B. White had defended and befriended the *i:laponathli:* for twenty-seven years. He had observed at close hand their tourist attraction economy, the creation of their Tamiami Trail camps, and the hunting, frogging, and crop picking by which they had made their living independent of the government. At the end of his career he commented on their commendable initiative: "Faced with a situation, these people had been able to protect themselves and prove their economy" (U.S. Congress 1954:1134).

CHAPTER 12

The *i:laponathli:* as Hosts

[They] open their homes and gardens for gain.

Ethel Cutler Freeman (1938)

In 1971 Sturtevant gave an overview of the *i:laponathli:'* tourist activities: "For many decades Seminole families have successfully exploited the tourist market in large part on their own initiative, with the production of craft goods and the operation of souvenir stores and 'exhibition villages' and by a type of theatrical performance called 'alligator wrestling'" (1971:121).

The accessibility of the "commercial" village attractions to Miami's tourists was of paramount importance to their enormous success. A 1989 study on the anthropology of tourism has defined "leisured mobility" in five hypothetical types of activities that draw tourists to an attraction: tourism that is ethnic, cultural, historical, environmental, and recreational (Smith 1989:4).

The Seminole village attractions appear at first glance to fall into the category of ethnic tourism, but Miami and Silver Springs were not "hard to reach" destinations that only a limited number of tourists would choose to visit, as ethnic tourism is defined. Cultural tourism defined most accurately the *i:laponathli:'* position in their original tourist market that made them so viable a commodity. It involves a tourist destination where picturesque local color and quaint customs prevail. The destination should be accessible from tourist centers and capable of drawing "large numbers of visitors . . . for the very purpose of observing and photographing" (ibid.:5).

The anthropological study of tourism is little more than a decade old (Nunez 1989:265). It has shown that "tourism is especially favored where significant segments of the [ethnic] population have minimal education or ethnic skills" (Smith 1989:xi). Certainly these qualifications would have applied to the *i:laponathli:*, coming directly as they did from a tradition of hunting, gathering, and gardening practices.

James L. Glenn had remarked on the *i:laponathli:'* tourist attraction economy at the opening ceremonies of the Tamiami Trail in 1928: "Their own private folkways have a cash value that must be bewildering" (Tebeau 1957:65). At the attractions these Native Americans were not required to have much physical contact with the tourists. Phil James of Coppinger's Village (1917–22) recalled that the *i:laponathli:* would "mill around with people and talk to them in broken English and get tips" (James 1980). Alan Davis of Musa Isle (1922–32) wrote in 1980, "They'd just sit in their huts and stare and the white people would just stare at them. . . . [A tourist would] go up there and talk to them and they'd be just as mum. The Indians wouldn't say one word." He further noted, "All [the Indian] did was sit in his hut. He didn't do [anything] except sleep and eat." Manager Nellie Campbell recalled (1981b), "They didn't relate to tourists at all. Sometimes a tourist would get too chummy and sit on a platform and they'd shove him off!" Ruth Holloway, a cook at Musa Isle in the 1920s, recalled (1981), "Every one of them, I think, had an old phonograph, and they used to lay around in their huts and play records." Sturtevant observed while conducting field work in 1952, "Guided tours move from monkeys to birds to Indians to alligators, while the Seminole occupants of the 'Indian Village' ignore the gawking whites" (1967:76).

Theron Nunez, a pioneer in the study of anthropological tourism, noted that the interaction between the host group and the tourists is "almost always marked by degrees of social distance and stereotyping. . . . The greater the ethnic and cultural distance between the host and tourist personnel, the greater the confusion and misunderstanding the two groups are likely to encounter and the less natural they are likely to act" (1989:271).

Certainly there was a great contrast between the cosmopolitan tourists from the Northeast and the *i:laponathli:*' tribal traditions learned in their distant Everglades camps. These deep cultural contrasts produced an aspect of the ugly American in downtown Miami, observed by Glenn in the 1930s: "The tourists will talk both loudly and freely about the damn funny clothes and the damn dirty pots, and some brute will grab the blouse of an Indian wife and yell, 'Hey Bill—want a squaw?' The husband of the wife will see what damn fools these tourists are, but will ignore it" (1982:102).

Exploitation in the tourist attractions deserves discussion. According to my research, the *i:laponathli:* as a people did not feel exploited, but incidents of out-and-out exploitation did occur. "Forward to the Soil" comes to mind as a most audacious example.

Cory Osceola was personally involved in a case of exploitation. As a young man in 1922, he had lost an arm in a railroad accident. A few years later, he attended an exposition at the Arkansas State Fair with a group of *i:laponathli:* from Musa Isle. A white friend from Miami was visiting in Arkansas and came to the fair to see the Seminoles from home. She was shocked when the barker related that Osceola's arm had been bitten off by an alligator! Cory himself was furious. The friend felt that this incident made him refuse to participate in any future out-of-town events (Higgens 1982).

Stirling noted in his 1936 study that "the camp owners use all manners of persuasion and threats to keep the Indians in the camps and prevent them from returning home. It is often necessary for them to sneak out of the camps in the middle of the night if they wish to leave" (9). While this information is sensational, it is also suspect, as he has not identified either the attraction personnel or the *i:laponathli:* informants. Further, there has been no documentation located to support such claims. As Musa Isle foreman Alan Davis (1980) explained from his experience, "The Indians were free to go any time they wanted to go. They weren't there by compulsion. They came because they wanted to." Seeming to echo Davis's statement, L. Mike Osceola (1982), who had lived in attractions since childhood, said that the *i:laponathli:* families "were there because they wanted to be there."

Neither can blame be placed on the managers of the villages, except perhaps Lasher's overcompetitive spirit and bouts of alcoholism. Henry Coppinger, Jr., was a member in good standing of Hanson's Seminole Indian Association (Coppinger Papers 1951). Nellie Campbell, Musa Isle owner and manager from 1932, was a member of the prestigious and influential Miami Women's Club, which had long been an advocate of Seminole welfare projects. She recalled that a group of club members interested in such projects were strongly opposed to the tourist attraction's Seminole villages, such as hers at Musa Isle, and made their displeasure known to her. Mrs. Campbell (1981b) replied to the chairwoman of the Indian Committee, Mrs. Hicks Allen, "The Indians on the Trail were surely not as well off as the ones in the Musa Isle camp." Campbell related that they calmed down, and she did not hear any more about it.

In the 1880 field study of ethnographer Clay MacCauley, he noted, "Laziness is not countenanced among the Seminole. He is a worker and not a loafer" (1887:503). Yet, Stirling, Davis, and James have all noted that the Indians in the tourist attraction camps (most assuredly they meant the men) "have nothing to do." Did a major cultural change occur in the decades of the tourist attractions, or were the observations of these men based too strongly on the Christian work ethic? The *i:laponathli:* were acutely aware of their job description in the attractions (they were to be in the camp for exhibition purposes) and demanded compensation for additional work (Davis 1980). If they were hired to be visible in the village at prescribed times while a boatload or busload of tourists were on hand, then that is what they did. Their other time might be read as "doing nothing" to an outsider.

The women were consistently hard at work making clothing to be worn and craft items to be sold. They were still responsible for shopping and cooking the meals. A man whittling on a piece of wood might be seen as "having nothing to do," but he might sell the item he was working on the next day. Male carvers were responsible for producing a significant amount of the souvenir crafts made of soft cypress wood, such as the toy canoes, knives, spears, and tomahawks that were sold from the attractions' stores. As the Florida Writers' Project noted in 1941, "Practically every Indian owns a sharp pocket knife and the older men are particularly skillful at using these in woodcarving" (30).

Continuing the discussion of the role of children in the attractions, Glenn was of the opinion that "the only home some of these children have is this cynosure of exhibition and sensation" (1982:104). Children "begging" is frequently mentioned by visitors. Alan Davis (1980) temporarily stopped the children at Musa Isle on the premise that he "didn't want the Indians to think that they would have to beg for anything." However, the children knew that the tourists were a soft touch and this was easy money, so it continued. Ethel Cutler Freeman wrote in 1941, "[The] Tiger children at Musa Isle beg for money, rattle jelly glasses to tourists. They are cute and would naively come back and proudly show that they had .50 and .25 cents, though their parents told them not to ask for money" (1941a).

The earning power of the children in the tourist attractions takes on serious economic importance when compared with a study conducted in Sri Lanka by the Ecumenical Coalition on Third World Tourism. Based in Bangkok, the coalition found that "children who 'beg' at airports and attractions often earn more cash in one day than their farmer-fishermen parents can earn in a month" (Smith 1989:9).

I:laponathli: parents could be accused of exploiting their children for photo tip money in the attractions. Their children posed with perfumed and lipsticked women and bewhiskered men, enduring unwanted hugs and kisses for the tips that would come. One incidence was reported of a child at Musa Isle who was severely, physically reprimanded by her mother for not asking tourists for money when her photo was taken. The child's income potential, like that of the Sri Lankan children, doubtless constituted a significant portion of the family's gross earnings (Goodwin 1946; White 1946).

Observers of the Seminole culture in the 1930s were anxious to relate the effects of acculturation on the *i:laponathli:*. Some believed that the Indians were losing their native ways and were glad, seeing this as "progress" which put them on their way to being acculturated. Others blamed the attractions for commercializing the Indians and making them insensitive. It was generally assumed that their traditions were lost as well. Still other critics commented that the *i:laponathli:* were acculturating the wrong elements from the dominant society. The "bad" Indian was once again the one at the tourist attraction.

In addition to the immediate need for cash, the *i:laponathli:* received some long-term benefits from their participation in the tourist attractions. Foremost is the market that was created for commercial crafts, while patchwork clothing was retained and continued its development. The importance of wearing native clothing in the tourist attraction can be seen in the contract for the exhibition of Seminoles at Marineland in 1941. The contract stipulated, "when before the public, The Indians shall always wear their complete tribal costume" (Tolstoy 1941).

Miami's "Seminole" villages were also of importance for on-the-job training. According to Nunez's study of the effects of tourism, "Traditionally prestigious individuals may be successful innovators when a community is undergoing gradual, orderly change, but 'culturally marginal' individuals appear to become successful innovators when a community is undergoing periods of 'rapid, stressful change'." It is a time when "cultural marginal individuals, being less conservative, perhaps more imaginative, may assume positions of leadership and may become successful innovators during periods of accelerated, disquieting change" (1989:268). Thus tourism had been found to occur among ethnic peoples during periods of rapid change, such as the *i:laponathli:'* economic trials early in the twentieth century.

Nunez identifies "marginal men" evolving as leaders from stressful situations such as the *i:laponathli:* had experienced. He defines a marginal man as "an individual who differs from some cultural norm or norms and who behaves and is treated accordingly" (ibid.:269). Important *i:laponathli:* marginal men would have been Cory Osceola, his brother William McKinley Osceola, and Josie Billie. Literate and seeking far more acculturated skills than most of their peers, these men were ambitious and authoritative. They were willing to place themselves in positions outside the norm in order to meet the demands of a situation created outside the control of their own culture but affecting its welfare.

In *i:laponathli:* society, deviancy from the norm could be punishable by death. All of these marginal men felt at times that someone was fixing medicine against them (Davis 1980). Cory and Juanita Osceola were prime examples. It will be recalled that the couple was married at the Musa Isle Village rather than traditionally at the Green Corn Dance, and their first child, Tahama, was the first *i:laponathli:* child born in a Miami hospital (*Miami Daily News* 1925). Their son, O. B. White Osceola, Sr., translated for his mother, "Mom and Dad almost got murdered by the Indians too, when they did that," showing the thin line which innovators walked in those days (Juanita Osceola 1985).

Based on Nunez's study, these marginal men could also be termed "culture brokers." A culture broker is a marginal man who is able to use his marginal qualities to his advantage. In particular, Cory Osceola emerges as the most influential culture broker. His pursuits appear to demonstrate that "entrepreneurship, for example, may be more adaptive than traditional economic subsistence pursuits. The marginal individual is one who may be psychologically inclined or motivated to cope with anxieties creatively" (Nunez 1989:269).

Cory Osceola had become literate and learned his figures as a young man. A retired schoolteacher, remembered only as the "Guava Lady" (she always brought some to the village when it was in season), was responsible for teaching him (Juanita Osceola 1985). Due to his physical handicap, traditional subsistence pursuits would have been difficult or at least a hindrance, but we also know that he let little get in his way. He was seen adroitly poling a canoe in the movie *Wind Across the Everglades* (Schulberg 1958). Physically he may have been challenged, but as a culture broker he could surpass his peers. In the capacity of headman, he regularly organized groups of *i:laponathli:* families for the attraction and exposition trips, handled salaries, purchased crafts along the Tamiami Trail, and managed the attraction's gift shop. As a field foreman, he hired hands for seasonal planting and picking. As a line boss, he oversaw the unloading of trains in Opa Locka. As a tribal leader, he consulted with the *i:laponathli:* Council and with its lawyer, O. B. White, and corresponded with Washington officials (Pete Osceola, Sr., 1983; Juanita Osceola 1985; O. B. White Osceola 1987; West 1987b; Johns and Cypress 1996).

Through decades that could have been a deep economic depression to these Native Americans, the tourist attractions served as a transitional environment, while as hosts to generations of tourists, the *i:laponathli:* reaped the benefits of "cultural tourism" for most of the twentieth century.

CHAPTER 13

Seminole Tourism Comes of Age

Ecotourism is the buzzword this year.

Sylvia Berman, president, Greater Hollywood Chamber of Commerce, in Bowers 1998

Indian participation at Musa Isle and Coppinger's Pirate's Cove saw a resurgence in the early 1940s during World War II. By the 1950s, however, the attractions generally supported only an extended family who lived permanently on the premises on a seasonal basis. According to Sturtevant, it was competition from the Indian-operated tourist attractions along the Tamiami Trail and new ones that opened on the Hollywood Reservation along U.S. 441 that reduced the number of Indians seeking employment in the city tourist attractions (1971:122).

The death knell tolled in the 1960s for the pioneer businesses of Musa Isle and Coppinger's Pirate's Cove (sold and renamed Tropical Paradise) as Miami's new expressway system sealed off easy access to these riverfront properties. Musa Isle closed in 1964 and Tropical Paradise in 1969 (Kleinberg 1985; Wardlow 1969). Thus two of Miami's earliest, most popular, and longest operating tourist attractions, the sites where the *i:laponathli:* developed a new economy, became history. But tourism was around to stay and is "the most important and most typical Florida Seminole economic activity of the 20th century" (Sturtevant 1997).

The tourist economy created by the *i:laponathli:* has remained remarkably consistent in its original form. Most of the elders and middle-aged baby boomers in the late 1990s were residents of area tourist attractions in the 1950s and 1960s at the sites of the original attractions of Musa Isle and Coppinger's or at Silver Springs. Others were associated with the later attractions of Tropical Hobbyland (Miami), the Hollywood Chimpanzee Farm (Dania Cutoff Canal), Aquaglades (Dania), Pippin Park (Dania Cutoff Canal), the *Jungle Queen* Seminole Village (New River, Fort Lauderdale), and numerous less-established Seminole villages on New River for sightseeing boats (*Abeona, Miss Everglades*). Still others recalled living in relatives' villages along the Tamiami Trail. The older generation tended to hold a strongly nostalgic view of their life-style in the attractions. They considered activities related to the tourist attractions to be a significant part of their cultural heritage.

However, there is an astonishing economic contrast between then and more recent tribal economics. "Ten years ago, we wrestled alligators, made a few dolls and sang songs for the tourists. We've come from the wheel age to the jet age in ten years," recounted Max Osceola (Panther), Seminole tribal councilman and major entrepreneur in 1983 (*Miami Herald* 1983). But greater prosperity was in store. In 1997, the Seminole Tribe approved a fiscal year 1998 budget of $127,881,000.

It was not always so. In the 1950s, those Seminoles residing on the federal reservations were encouraged to incorporate and govern themselves, following the threat of tribal termination under Senate Bill 2747 and House Bill 7321. The organizers of the future Seminole Tribe of Florida did not have enough money to send their representatives to meetings at the state capital in Tallahassee, much less to Washington. The impoverished tribal officials were desperate. They decided in 1956 under the leadership of Bill Osceola (Bird) and with the aid of the Friends of the Seminoles organization, based in Fort Lauderdale, to host a rodeo as a fund raiser. Donations of starter money, goods, and services were solicited and received from community organizations and friends who were long-time Seminole supporters (West 1995a). The event was successful and has become part of the tribe's tourism package.

The Seminole Tribe of Florida was federally recognized in 1957. Ironically, the first major industry created in 1959 by the Bureau of Indian Affairs for the new tribe was a tourist attraction, "Okalee Indian Village." Okalee was a classic Seminole Indian attraction, complete with alligator wrestling pits, zoo, wedding reenactments at festivals, and an ultramodern crafts building. Ironically as well, it was located near the former site of the old Seminole Agency Building in Hollywood where Special Commissioner James L. Glenn and others had bemoaned what they perceived as the demeaning exploitation of the Seminoles on exhibition.

In the 1950s, the *i:laponathli:* along the Trail had initiated a strong separatist campaign when the government's termination hearings for the Seminoles were under way (see Kersey 1996:175–99). The government understood that there were fundamental differences between the Florida Indians called "Seminoles," but until the end the government's negotiators hoped to resolve these differences, viewed by Washington as factionalism that surely could be negotiated.

Miccosukee leader Jimmie Billie (Bird) found Musa Isle a convenient location in which to live with his family while coordinating the Miccosukee Tribal Movement. It was perhaps there that a major publicity stunt was organized to draw public attention to the *i:laponathli:* separatists. A contingency of Miccosukees went to pre-Communist Cuba to meet with Fidel Castro in July 1959. They sought his public recognition, which they were granted, much to the displeasure of the United States, then entering into tense diplomatic relations with that country.

These Trail Indians—whose families had comprised a large percentage of the pioneer employees at Miami tourist attractions and who were also the antigovernment sympathizers who opened their own attraction villages along the Tamiami Trail—were finally recognized by the U.S. government as separate from the Seminoles. This major obstacle out of the way and with significant stipulations to protect their culture, such as their own education system, they formally organized as the Miccosukee Tribe of Indians of Florida on January 11, 1962.

But during the termination hearings of the 1950s, additional political-ideological factions within the *i:laponathli:* enclave became apparent. The family of William McKinley Osceola declared itself independent. Its members vehemently opposed the newly organized Miccosukee Tribe for its lack of traditional values. Head of yet a larger group of Independent Seminoles, Cory Osceola was the active political leader of nonreservation *i:laponathli:* in Collier County, operating from his tourist attraction village on the Tamiami Trail in Naples until his death in 1978.

Seminole tribal tourism languished during the 1970s and 1980s because of insufficient funding. The Miccosukee Tribe, on the other hand, threw all of its meager resources into tourism. By the 1970s they had formulated an intense public relations program spearheaded by Lee and Stephen, sons of chairman Buffalo Tiger. The Tiger brothers were the spokesmen for a media blitz that announced the new Miccosukee tribal presence to a public who had heard only of the Seminoles. Further popularizing the small tribe was the brothers' rock band, "Tiger Tiger." The tribe continued its campaign for visibility by publicizing its sovereignty. It opened and operated the Miccosukee Embassy on property on the Miami River near downtown Miami, not far from the former locations of Musa Isle and Coppinger's Tropical Gardens.

In the 1970s the concept of cigarette shops on tax-free Indian reservation land was first introduced in the United States by the Florida Seminoles. "High-stakes bingo" was the next novel enterprise that the Seminoles implemented on their sovereign land. As their coffers began to swell, the tribe also began to make corporate donations to political candidates who could offer assistance to its upwardly mobile members. The long-impoverished Seminole Tribe began to flex its muscles as a sovereign nation (see Kersey 1996).

The billion dollar tribe has erected an impressive four-story glass and steel office building topped by a heliopad at corporate headquarters on the Hollywood Reservation. It maintains its own newspaper, broadcasting department and web site with a marketplace (www.seminoletribe.com). Lobbyists are supported at the state and federal levels to protect the prized reservation lands from such hazards as chemical infiltration from the U.S. Sugar Corporation in the Big Cypress or to protect the tribe's prized cattle industry from the effects of the state's Flood Control Division. Meanwhile, tribal leaders view neither "smoke shops" nor gaming as permanent situations, knowing that a high court ruling could take them away. Then the tribe would have to fall back on such revenues as cattle production (nineteenth largest producer of calves in the nation) and citrus (world's number one producer of lemons). It has additional diversifications: a turtle farm, a rope-making factory for Seminole brand rodeo lanyards, land leasing, and an airplane factory, with additional projects in the planning stages. However, it is "smoke shops" and "high stakes bingo" which have made the tribe the major corporation it is today.

Tribal tourism was thriving. Far from being abandoned in the wake of new economic boons, the tribal financial backing of old and new tourist venues saw a great resurgence from 1990 to 2000. The revenues of smoke shops and gaming are being reinvested in ventures that can compete with the world's best examples of cultural attractions and ecotourism.

In Florida near the end of the century, ecotourism was the buzz word of the day. It was popular with European tourists, who were especially interested in "the State's natural attractions, such as the Everglades" (Hutt 1997a). The Seminole Tribe's ecotourism ventures promote cultural activities such as crafts production and sales, alligator wrestling, zoo keeping, the wearing of patchwork clothing, canoe making and canoeing demonstrations, traditional foods, and the telling of Seminole legends.

The person who was the consistent advocate of tribal tourism was Chairman James E. Billie (Bird), an interesting case in point. Billie was born in the early 1940s in a local tourist attraction, the Hollywood Chimpanzee Farm—a fact that he relishes. A Vietnam veteran and a shrewd politician, he is also well known as an entertainer and a consummate alligator wrestler. In the 1970s, prior to taking up politics, he was manager of the struggling, financially strapped Seminole Okalee Indian Village. He also traveled throughout the state and country with a crated alligator, performing wrestling engagements. He pinned down a 275-pound alligator in less than two minutes to gain a place in the Guinness Book of World Records, as seen on the "Guinness Game" television show (McClare 1979). That same year, shortly after his first election as chairman, he was asked how things were going. "Well," he said thoughtfully, "It's just like alligator wrestling. You never know which way they're going to come at you!" (Billie 1980). Billie has always mixed alligator wrestling and politics. In 1982 the *Miami Herald* quoted him as saying, "I like to catch a fresh gator or two . . . if I'm going to wrestle for a congressman." Over sixty years have passed since Roy Nash's recommendation that "Indian Villages for show purposes" should be banned (Nash 1931:44). In 1998, the Seminole Tribe reopened the fully renovated Seminole Okalee Indian Village, the site of the annual Seminole Tribal Fair, Pow Wow, and PRCA Rodeo, now in its thirty-sixth year. The newly renovated fairgrounds and rodeo arena offer a first-class entertainment facility with covered seating. Seminole foods, *chickee* craft booths, Seminole clothing contests, alligator wrestling, and craft and dance demonstrations continue to promote Seminole culture in this highly successful educational event which draws the entire Indian population from all communities. Over the years this event has incorporated demonstrations of dancers from the Plains, the southwest, and the Great Lakes and other entertainers, as well as championship powwows with large cash prizes.

The Seminole tribal prosperity was shared in the 1990s by sizably increasing quarterly, then monthly dividends which were received by every tribal member—man, woman, and child. In 1998 the monthly dividend peaked at $2,000. However, in light of this prosperity, some of the older, conservative members of the Seminole Tribe feared that crafts and culture would be forgotten in the race to obtain all of the material goods available to modern-day households. Satellite dishes, gold jewelry, designer clothing, and a wide variety of vehicles seemed a real threat to the making of sweet grass baskets and patchwork clothing and demonstrations of alligator wrestling, which have been so much a part of Seminole family life in the twentieth century.

Anxious about the effects that this economic turn of events might have on Seminole culture, Chairman Billie, then in his fifth term of office, created educational programs that stress language, history, and culture at the Tribe's Ah-Fach-Kee School (K–12) in Big Cypress. Chairman Billie stated at the opening of the tribe's Sheridan Hotel in Tampa, "I don't want to lose the old ways, but we can't turn back the clock" (*Orlando Sentinel* 1987).

But numerous families continued to practice tourism. Individuals in both the Seminole and Miccosukee tribes and among the handful of Independent Seminoles continued to be involved in the tourist economy, where a definite continuum exists. Tourists eager to experience ecotourism and cultural tourism continued to cruise in boats such as the *Jungle Queen*, still making daily runs up New River in Fort Lauderdale to an "Indian Village." There, they could photograph the Seminoles, purchase unique crafts and patchwork, and witness alligator wrestling among cages of exotic birds and monkeys. A "Seminole wedding" was included as part of the festivities at "Bobby's Seminole Village" at the Seminole Tribe's Tampa Reservation, and Jack Tiger Tail's gesturing likeness pointed the way off I-75 to the Seminole Tribe's popular Big Cypress attraction, Kissimmee Billie Swamp Safari. Both tribes offered Indian village venues and airboat rides. One enterprising Seminole family, Judy (Panther) and Pete Baker (Judy is the granddaughter of Sam Huff), had success marketing a Seminole village concession as part of a larger attraction. Their proposal for a model Seminole village on the Kissimmee River in conjunction with Swampland Tours was endorsed by the Conservation Center for Lake Okeechobee–Kissimmee–Everglades Education (C-OKEE) (Valentine 1997). Miccosukee alligator wrestler Kenny Cypress (Bird) made international news when his head was pinned in an alligator's mouth during his wrestling show at the Miccosukee Festival. Boosted to celebrity status in the hospital, he was soon back in the ring (*Orlando Sentinel* 1998).

The Columbus Sesquicentennial—a controversial event for Native Americans—supplied a reason for the Seminole Tribe to enter into another tourist venue. Using a concept of the late James Jumper and with the backing of the Seminole Tribe and Chairman Billie, the tribe opted to celebrate the Sesquicentennial in a positive manner by applauding their survival and the survival of other tribes for the past 500 years. The Seminoles hosted what was then the largest powwow east of the Mississippi River. Called Discover Native America, the annual event, which attracted hundreds of championship Native American dancers to compete for large cash prizes, premiered on the Hollywood Reservation in 1992. It then moved annually: to Orlando and Jacksonville, Florida; Nashville, Tennessee; St. Petersburg, Florida; and Atlanta, Georgia, for the Olympics in 1996.

The Miccosukee Tribe's continuing involvement in tourism created the summer Everglades Music and Crafts Festival, now in its thirty-first year, and a Miccosukee Arts and Music Festival held in December at their cultural base, the Miccosukee Indian Village, a year-round tourist attraction. The 635-member tribe was located on 333 acres adjoining Everglades National Park, but the 5.5-mile-long, 500-foot-wide strip was not technically reservation land. The Miccosukees hold it by a "special use permit" that will expire in 2014. They were in fact at the mercy of the U.S. Park Service, which was keeping them from building sixty-five homes on their land (Cypress 1998). The tribe made use of their popular December Arts Festival as a forum to collect signed petitions in support of the tribe's request to build the homes (Gehrke 1997). The tribe also took out full-page ads in Florida newspapers calling attention to their predicament on the weekend that Everglades National Park celebrated its fiftieth birthday with Vice President Gore in attendance (Miccosukee Tribe of Indians of Florida 1997). It is fortunate that they are now financially able to purchase their own land—they recently bought 800 acres abutting the Fakahatchee Strand in Collier County (Staats 1997b). With a newer gaming economy than the Seminole Tribe—but one gathering momentum— the Miccosukee Tribe operated a thriving "smoke shop" and an increasingly popular "high stakes bingo" parlor on the eastern end of the Tamiami Trail.

This small tribe, which continues to say "Just let us alone!" to the government, has some interesting political clout, and some of their wishes were being heard. Ironically, a key issue that they have raised affects the important Florida Everglades. The tribe has demanded that the State of Florida scrap the poorer water standards set for the highly publicized Everglades restoration, an $835 million project, and meet the Miccosukee

Tribe's advanced water standards in the widely publicized controversy. The Miccosukees were thus set to play a role in the preservation of Florida's $37.9 billion tourism industry.

Native American tourism was a hot topic on the Florida Gold Coast, and even the terminology often changed to keep up with this growing industry. While alligator wrestlers had to pull permits in order to take a 'gator across county lines legally, international tours destined for the Seminole and Miccosukee tourist attractions could be arranged through Lee Tiger and Associates, Inc. In the 1980s Tiger promoted his tourism interests as the "Goodwill Ambassador of the Everglades." In the 1990s, as a consultant to the Seminole Tribe, he marketed Seminole tribal tourism at such events as the annual International Tourism Exchange in Berlin where brochures read "Play Florida with the Real Natives" (*Okeechobee News* 1996). Marketing Native American interests, Tiger combined "eco" and "heritage" tourism to include the Tribe's Native American powwows (Jones 1997). In March 1997, the Seminole Tribe hosted an evening gala, "The Seminole Swamp Party," for the Florida Huddle, Florida's largest international tourism showcase held at the tribe's newly renovated Okalee Indian Village (Tom Gallagher 1997). Tiger also touted the worldwide demand for the tribe's "eco-multi-cultural" tourism venues at the World Travel Market in London, where over 60,000 delegates "represented every major country in the world" and in 1998 at the Mid-Atlantic Workshop and Travel Seminar in Reykjavik, Iceland. He noted (1997) that "the State of Florida as well as Greater Fort Lauderdale tourism have created a partnership with Seminole Tourism in order to educate the travel industry worldwide of the unique and authentic tourist activities the Seminole Tribe now offers."

On August 21, 1997, the fortieth anniversary of the Seminole Tribe of Florida was celebrated with the opening of the world-class Ah-Tah-Thi-Ki Museum, "A Place to Learn, a Place to Remember." Building One was a showcase of late nineteenth-century tribal culture and history. The tribe had just sued U.S. Interior Secretary Bruce Babbitt, hoping to expand its operations to include casino-style gambling. To offset any negative press and to soften the state in regard to the Seminoles' gaming interests, the tribe organized a million dollar publicity campaign to introduce Florida's population to the tribe. Television spots and full-page ads in all major Florida newspapers downplayed gaming interests while emphasizing the tribe's contributions to the state's economy and listing its varied diversifications such as cattle and citrus, highlighting real people, Seminole cattlemen and teachers. As the tribe's newest tourist destination,

Ah-Tah-Thi-Ki Museum's grand gala opening showcased the tribal anniversary. The positive commitment of this facility to Seminole heritage further served to provide a subliminal contrast to the tribe's gaming interests, which, ironically, were what made the multimillion dollar museum a reality.

With substantial growth slated in the future, the Ah-Tah-Thi-Ki Museum complex features a 1.2-mile-long environmental boardwalk through a cypress hammock and a living Seminole village. The museum was enthusiastically included in Broward County's latest tourist promotion, the "Shore Thing," which encouraged cruise boat visitors to stay on land for a few more days with free accommodations and free admission to the museum (Hutt 1997b).

There were many things to see and do on the Seminole reservations. The tribe's Kissimmee Billie Swamp Safari a few miles from the museum offered hunting, camping, and exotic animal photo safaris by swamp buggy. A restaurant, the Swamp Water Café, served such Everglades fare as frog legs and alligator tail. The Seminole Tribe of Florida, Inc. (the business corporation) reopened Seminole Okalee Indian Village at Hollywood in 1998. The Ah-Tah-Thi-Ki Museum opened a branch facility at that location called Okalee Museum. Independent Seminole Bobby Henry leased and operated Bobby's Seminole Indian Village attraction from the Seminole Tribe on their Tampa Reservation, which featured daily craft and alligator wrestling demonstrations as well as annual cultural festivals. There were also popular music festivals that brought in national talent to the Seminole reservations' rodeo arenas.

Statistics from Nicki E. Grossman, president of Greater Fort Lauderdale Convention and Visitors Bureau, showed that "A lot of tourists are coming for non-traditional reasons. One hot item is ecological and cultural tourism. They're coming to see the Everglades and the Seminole Indians" (Varma 1997). Lee Tiger commented, "The Seminoles have eco-cultural activities that are unique and like no other in the world" (Bowers 1998). Indeed, a listing of the visitors to Ah-Tah-Thi-Ki Museum in the first two weeks of operation (keeping in mind that the museum is in the middle of the Big Cypress) included guests from a variety of countries: England, Spain, Puerto Rico, Belize, South Africa, Denmark, Germany, Italy, Venezuela, Switzerland, Iceland, Hungary, France, Sweden, New Zealand, Czech Republic, Romania, Holland, Belgium, and Australia (West 1997).

Thus the *i:laponathli:* have a strong continuum of commitment to tourism, and tourism is seeing a revived interest in the *i:laponathli:* and their

Everglades homeland, an economy that these enterprising Native Americans have experienced and refined to suit their life-style and the tourists' needs for nine decades.

Writing on the 1995 White House Conference on Travel and Tourism, Tandy Young (Choctaw), president of the Native American Travel Service and Tourism Center, commented, "Indian reservations are tourism goldmines and tribes are foolish not to make the most of it" (Young 1996:5). Pioneers in tourism and first in tribal gaming seem to be a winning combination. Tribal commitments to cultural and "eco" tourism will play a major role in keeping these Native Americans in touch with their environment and heritage, while their gaming proceeds will fund projects that those early pioneers of the Miami tourist attractions would never have thought possible. As other tribes gear up to reap tourist dollars on their reservations, the Florida Seminoles and Miccosukees are way ahead of the game.

CHAPTER 14

Tourism Rocks

Gaming, as the strong, new tourism venture, continued to escalate for the Tribes. However, the threat of a reversal of the Indian Gaming Regulatory Act that would take away the "new buffalo" was always in the back of the tribal politicians' minds. As a result, economic diversification continued in the 1990s and into the new century, becoming a real and practiced strategy. To that end, Chairman James E. Billie (Bird clan) made investments in Nicaragua. A herd of Seminole cattle was established there that opened up trade possibilities from their out-of-country base with other countries—even Communist Cuba—where trade was blocked by U.S.-based interests. It was in Nicaragua that the tribe had their first connection with a Hard Rock enterprise, buying an interest in a Legends Hotel and the Hard Rock Live Hotel in Managua. In Florida they opened Tribal-owned Micco Aircraft Company in Ft. Pierce and established new agriculture and aquaculture venues on the Brighton and Big Cypress Reservations. Of these outreaching economic ventures Chairman Billy explained, "We're just learning how to spend money. And the only way to learn is you've got to have it in the first place" (Yari 1999:50).

The Seminoles and Miccosukees continued to build their empires based on the newer types of tourist leisure activities: gaming, sports, recreation, and hospitality, with gaming providing the maximum of their tourism dollars. "We're all in the entertainment business . . . looking for people to come in on their free time and spend their expendable money," said Jeff Purcell, marketing director for Miccosukee Gaming (Snel 1998).

The Miccosukee Tribe was gaining an identity by bringing important sports meets like championship boxing to South Florida and bankrolling large, pricey suites at Pro Player Stadium. Their logo, "Miccosukee Indian Gaming," was prominently displayed in advertisements at sports venues such as the nationally televised Orange Bowl and Miami Heat games. Meanwhile, they were offering $17 million monthly for gaming prizes. The Seminole Tribe also used national sports venues as a marketing tool to advertise their gaming operations.

In 1999 the Miccosukees added a $46 million, five-star, 302-room hotel to their gaming facility, Miccosukee Resort and Gaming, turning it into a real entertainment destination. Because the Miccosukee Tribe of Indians of Florida bases its existence on cultural traditions, its governing body distributes a greater share of earnings to the population than the Seminole Tribe distributes to its members (West 2007a:16).

The Seminoles opened a casino on the Brighton Reservation on the northwest corner of Lake Okeechobee in December 1999. That enterprise was followed in February 2000 by the tribe's fifth casino, the Coconut Creek Casino, which was constructed on a small plot of sovereign land—just under five acres—that the tribe had received in exchange for road easements along U.S. Highway 441 in front of the Hollywood Reservation. A similar situation existed when the state ramrodded construction of the Florida Turnpike right through the Hollywood Reservation, dividing it in half. The Seminoles, who at the time had no political clout, received some compensation through tiny, seemingly useless parcels of gifted land along U.S. 441. In the 1980s, they found a use for them. They hauled in trailers and set up drive-through smoke shops on this federal trust land.

Then the Seminole Tribe announced that plans for a $400 million Hard Rock hotel, casino, retail shopping center, and entertainment complex were underway. It would be located on the Seminoles' urban Hollywood Reservation, encompassing the land where the Seminole Okalee Indian Village was located.

Okalee is deeply rooted in the memory of much of the population. There, early tribal politicians held their first rodeo on a shoestring budget in the 1950s. Okalee was the site developed by the government in the

1960s for the newly recognized Seminole Tribe's tourist attraction, Seminole Okalee Indian Village. Year after year the elder generation of tribal officers, councilmen, and councilwomen continued to maintain the (unfortunately obsolete) tourist village theme with ingenuity and hard work, periodically redesigning it, patching up the cracked concrete, re-thatching it, and sinking money into it that they didn't have to waste. This was done in order to preserve the tourist and tribal site—utilized most actively as the location of the tribe's annual Seminole Tribal Fair and Rodeo—which had become an active part of their cultural and (theoretical) economic heritage.

In 2000, therefore, tribal citizens were elated with Okalee's complete modernization, which was made possible through their gaming revenues. The old Okalee was leveled and reconstructed on a larger scale. Improved infrastructure and the modern design and lighting of the Rodeo Arena, Living Village, huge Show Amphitheater, and a new branch of the Ah-Tah-Thi-Ki Museum—which included an expensive, state-of-the-art alligator-wrestling pit—contributed to Okalee's new, Disney-like appearance. It was everything that they had ever dreamed of, everything that they could have hoped for. Then, with the newness still apparent, they were told it was all to be demolished to build "Hard Rock." At Seminole Fair in February 2001, many were incredulous and angry (West 2001).

The tribe was receiving $300 million in profits each year, mostly from gaming. The dividend for each tribal member, now a "tribal citizen," was steady at $2,000 a month ($96,000 a year for a family of four), but the people wanted more. Their politicians promised them $3,000 a month by the end of the year ($144,000 a year for a family of four).

By 2001 James Billie had been chairman for twenty-two years, shooting from the hip, making decisions that he felt would best benefit the tribe, a seeming "Third World Nation" on the rise. Billie had taken the tribe from a $500,000 budget in 1979 to a $650 million budget in 2001. But suddenly changes were afoot as accusations of a personal, financial, and political nature began to fly around the head of James Billie. Alerted tribal citizens began to realize that they needed to pay personal attention to their tribe and their own destiny . . . look what was happening to Okalee. In a major political upheaval Chairman Billie was suspended by the political body.

In summer of 2001, the Hard Rock plans continued to escalate. But then, tribal citizens were provided with a pricey project overview, a thirteen-minute "virtual" film presented by Hollywood Council Representative Max B. Osceola Jr. (Panther clan). The session at the Hollywood Reservation auditorium began with Osceola asking a basic question,

"Hard Rock. Why is the Seminole Tribe going into it?" The project was to be funded by Merrill Lynch bonds to be paid back with income from the profitable venture itself (Frank 2001).

The ongoing investigation of Billie involved the federal government, the FBI, and the Indian Gaming Commission. As a result, the personal expenditures of all the tribal leaders were scrutinized for possible misuse of their discretionary accounts. Although Billie was acquitted of wrongdoing by the federal government, the Tribal Council and Board officers were warned to contain their spending or risk having their casinos shut down by the Indian Gaming Commission. The result has been a more professional business structure in all tribal departments. However, in the next election, politicians refused to place Billie's name on the ballot because of past transgressions. He became persona non grata on the reservations, with supporters meeting him in private, afraid of being seen in his company (West 2007a:16; Gallagher 2007:26).

The Tampa Hard Rock Hotel and Casino opened in March 2004 and the huge Hard Rock complex opened on the Hollywood Reservation in May 2004. The Hard Rocks are glitzy. Tourists and locals dress up for a grand night out at Hard Rock Hollywood. They race their cars into the huge multistoried parking garage and run to the elevators, passing through the tempting retail area of eye-catching shops and restaurants. Inside the casino, an astounding variety of rock memorabilia is exhibited in cases along the walls. All of the greats! Bands performing on several small, intimate stages amid the din of the gaming machines. Some Baby Boomers get up and dance. The hotel concierge tries to field a phone message over the music and the din of the slots.

This atmosphere seems totally incongruous with the simple ideals of the Florida Seminoles and Miccosukees discussed at the beginning of this book: the Everglades camps so close to nature, the quiet, circumspect elders, the pioneers of the Miami attractions. Generations of anthropologists, government surveys, historians, and the media have considered them on the "endangered list." Now they're *not*. They are now equipped with the financial and political clout to define their own destiny.

The Seminole Tribe presently employs more than 2,000 non-Indians and purchases more than $24 million a year in goods and services from more than 850 Florida vendors. In addition, the tribe pays $3.5 million in federal payroll taxes. In the 1960s, when Seminole tourism was at low ebb, tribal members made a poor person's living at best at the few tourist attractions and seasonal craft venues. while a few other craft makers supplied the sellers, spending hours making the baskets or patchwork clothing to sell. Most families barely made ends meet until the tribes' cigarette and gaming economy of the 1970s.

It has recently been revealed that James Billie went out on a limb to make that prosperity happen for his tribe. The Seminoles, like other tribes living on federal trust land, could not get conventional lenders such as banks to invest in their projects. The tribes had no collateral because the federal government owned their land. There were no organizations comparable to the Friends of the Seminole, whose philanthropic activities in the 1950s created the Seminole Acres Subdivision on the Hollywood Reservation by providing a revolving fund that individual Seminoles could tap into and pay back for homes donated and moved to the reservation or for building supplies for new homes (Jumper and West 2001:144–49). And the federal government was certainly not interested in investing in such a controversial operation as gaming, which was illegal in many states, including Florida. When Billie was elected in 1979, he quickly engineered a $3 million loan from a source that he never met but has recently identified as Florida Mafia boss Meyer Lansky. The tribe then built the first bingo hall on the Hollywood Reservation and let the money roll in. They paid off the lender's note in just six months. Billie watched proudly as "this world changed for the Seminole Tribe" (Gallagher 2007:28).

The Seminoles and Miccosukees want to be known as Florida Seminole or Miccosukee Indians, not "the Indians who invented Indian Gaming and got rich." For the tribes, gaming is just the means to an end, a way to remain Seminole or Miccosukee by utilizing this pot of gold, this "new buffalo," to build museums, to invest in more conventional businesses, to lobby for needs such as water quality in the Everglades, to create culture and language programs, to sponsor education and travel, and to train future Seminole and Miccosukee employees to operate the tribal enterprises and to serve on the Council and Board. Jessica Cattelino has shown in her recent Ph.D. dissertation, "High Stakes: Seminole Sovereignty in the Casino Era," that "Seminole economy and culture long have been co-produced, even as Seminoles pursued economic activities considered by outsiders to be assimilation, and then demonstrating several ways that casinos are (re)productive, not corrosive, of Seminole identity, community, and political authority" (Cattelino 2004:11). And the Seminole Tribe now has *seven* reservation-based casinos.

This is not a new concept, as the late Billy L. Cypress, then executive director of the Ah-Tah-Thi-Ki Museum, noted in a Broward County business magazine in 1996. "It seems funny that these things that somehow seem totally irrelevant or not related to our culture are helping to foot some of the bills. The tribe is just trying to exist and take advantage of its economic opportunity and hopefully take care of itself, its health and its education" (E. Davis 1996). And, in an updated interpretation, there is Max B. Osceola's quip: "We used to survive by hunting the game of the land. Now we survive by the Gaming in this land" (Lantigua 2007).

The image that the media paint of the tribes is all that is readily apparent to the man on the street. With the unprecedented economic success filling tribal coffers, less affluent populations living near the reservations often exhibit jealousy. Just the other day I was sitting in a homey eatery near Hollywood Reservation that is often patronized by tribal citizens. As if on cue, I overheard a man sitting near me say, "*These* Indians are getting *free* money! I have to work *hard* for *my* money!" (West 2007b).

Most non-Indians are totally unaware of the Seminoles' and Miccosukees' hardships that began with the three wars with the United States. In the twentiethth century they suffered hunger, culture lost without the means to make a living, and deaths due to lack of medical care. Do most Americans realize that living on a reservation with no infrastructure is a lot like living in an apartment with an absentee landlord and an unbreakable lifelong lease?

Other observers are sure that the financial boon of gaming will ruin the Seminole and Miccosukee cultures. Doesn't that sound familiar? That is, of course, up to the Seminole and Miccosukee people. That's their business. However, from the looks of the programs that are springing up, the culture is in viable hands. A case in point is Ah-Tah-Thi-Ki Museum. The world-class museum opened August 21, 1997. While it has been enjoyed by tourists from many countries, it had not until recently begun to serve as the focal point for tribal citizens. Now, under the leadership of Independent Seminole Cory Osceola's granddaughter, Tina M. Osceola, the museum is actively taking its place in the lives of the tribal citizens, as well as seeking professional status nationally as an American Association of Museums–accredited facility.

Thus, when I read the streaming tape on CNN the morning of December 7, 2006, it was exhilarating to learn that the Seminole Tribe of Florida had gone global, buying the London-based Rank Group's Hard Rock International, one of the most recognizable brands in the world, and paying nearly a billion dollars in the deal. Begun in London in 1971, the Hard Rock Cafés showcase what has been called the "largest collection of music memorabilia in the world," totaling seventy thousand pieces including rock stars' guitars and Madonna's black lace bustier. Talk about diversification. The Hard Rock venues give the Florida Seminoles an instant presence in forty-five countries. There are also four Hard Rock Hotels and two casinos worldwide, two on Seminole Reservations—Hollywood and Tampa—which opened in 2004. The Hard Rock purchase brings the tribe sixty-eight company-owned restaurants in the United States, Canada, Europe, Australia, and Puerto Rico. A headline proclaimed, "Seminoles make largest single corporate acquisition of American Indian tribe." Now that they own businesses from Spain to Japan, "The sun will always shine on Seminoles' Hard Rock Cafés," Max B. Osceola Jr., council representative from the Hollywood Reservation, enthusiastically proclaimed. "We are worldwide now and thinking outside the box" (Burnstein 2006; Suarez 2007:37). Florida Indians are firmly back in tourism again, now focusing on resort, hospitality, gaming, and retail ventures all over the world.

The Seminoles' Council Oak (on the Hollywood Reservation at Stirling Road and U.S. Highway 441) had been silent witness to the Seminoles' growth since the Hollywood Reservation's inception in 1925. It witnessed students' homework sessions, Girl Scout meetings, and the signatories as the tribe became self-governing and was federally recognized in 1957; now, nearing the fiftieth anniversary of that occasion, it again witnessed an important event, this time the formal closing of the Hard Rock International deal. Hollywood Council representative Max B. Osceola Jr., who had been at the federal recognition event as a child, projected, "Now main street [in the] business world knows you can do business with native tribes and make a profit" (Burnstein 2007b). AP business writer Jon Sainz noted of the Hard Rock transaction, "It marks the tribe's entry in the worldwide hospitality industry and gives the tribe's gaming operations a foothold in states where gambling is legal" (Sainz 2007).

Not gathering any dust, the Seminoles are currently planning another venture, the expansion of their Coconut Creek Casino northwest of Ft. Lauderdale to include a four-story, 1,500-room hotel, which will be the largest hotel in Broward County, with expanded casino, shops, restaurants, and offices on forty-four acres that they purchased surrounding the casino. To do this, they hope that the federal government will take the land for them as a trust property, rendering it sovereign and tax exempt (presently being opposed by the City of Coconut Creek). The tribe is also hoping for Las Vegas–style slot machines and table games in the future, which they may be able to negotiate with the state of Florida. With these plans as yet unresolved, the tribe's gaming CEO, James Allen, calls the project "a master plan, not a definite plan" (Burnstein 2007a).

In March 2007 the founding chairman of the Miccosukee Tribe of Indians of Florida, Buffalo Tiger, turned eighty-seven. A party was held for him by his son, musician and promoter Lee Tiger, at the Miccosukee Golf and Country Club in Kendall (southwest Miami). Lee's brother Stephen, of the band Tiger Tiger, had passed away six months earlier just after being awarded the Lifetime Achievement Award from the Native American Music Association at the Seminoles' Hollywood Hard Rock facility (West 2007c).

Meanwhile the Seminole Tribal elections were scheduled for May 2007. James Billie was planning a comeback but found that his bid for a place on the ballot to run for chairman (his former $330,000-a-year position) was once again denied by the Seminole politicians. He will have to wait another four years to try again. Meanwhile, he will continue to support his family by building *chickees*, a labor-intensive profession based on cultural tradition and in great demand with the "leisure and tourism" industry. Billie reflected on his life, "Every time in my life that I've gotten down financially, I went back to building *chickees*, and it brought me back up" (Gallagher 2007:26).

The Seminole Tribe no longer divulges the amounts of its dividends. The earnings have risen to a level that boosts a family's combined income to an impressive, newsworthy height, especially when set in bold headlines. Understandably, Seminole family income has now become a tribal privacy issue, as personal financial gains are no one's business but their own. Tribal citizens have been counseled to say only, "Generous!" when asked, "What's it up to now?" However, the latest figures published from recent leaks to newspapers and magazines place the dividend at $7,000 a month ($330,000 a year for a family of 4). And *yes* is the answer to an often-asked question: the Seminole and Miccosukees, like all United States citizens, pay personal income tax on their income.

It was not so long ago that the *i:laponathli* and the *ci:saponki:*, members of today's Seminole Tribe and Miccosukee Tribe of Indians of Florida, were the features of roadside attractions where a tourist could purchase a doll or watch an alligator being wrestled. Today the Florida Seminole and Miccosukee are still in the tourist attraction business. At first they could only bet on it, but now they can depend on it.

American Eagle. 1935. "Big Cypress Indians Aroused Hold Pow-Wow and Refuse to Recognize Peace Conference at West Palm Beach Between Government Agents and Indians of Small Group." April 11. Estero, Fla.: Koreshan Unity.

———. 1936. "Governor's Party Holds Powwow with Seminoles." February 27.

———. 1937. "Recounting a Bit of Trail History." April 8.

Anonymous. ca. 1928. Journal. Private collection, Coppinger Papers. Photocopy in the Seminole/Miccosukee Photographic Archive, Fort Lauderdale.

Applebaum. 1939. *New York World's Fair in Photographs*. The New-York Historical Society, New York City.

Bahl, George. 1900. Letter to J. E. Ingraham. November 22. Flagler Archives, Palm Beach.

Bartlett, Ellen. 1983. "Wrestler's peril in pit pays off." *Miami Herald*, February 22.

Bedell, Harriet M. 1933. Handwritten note on reverse of letter from Bishop John D. Wing, April 28. Bedell Papers, Historical Museum of Southern Florida, Miami, Fla. Photocopies, Seminole/Miccosukee Photographic Archive, Fort Lauderdale.

———. 1935. Price list, *The American Eagle*. September 26. Estero, Fla.: Koreshan Unity.

———. 1941. Glade Cross Mission newsletter. June 21. Bedell Papers, Historical Museum of Southern Florida, Miami, Fla.

Bellamy, Jeanne. 1980. "Sewell, the Chamber, and the Marketing of Miami." *Update* 7, no. 1 (February):2–5.

Berkhofer, Robert F., Jr. 1978. *The White Man's Indian*. New York: Vintage Books.

Biggers, L. Garland. 1936. "High Spots in the History of the Sun Dance." *Tropical Sun*, March 13. West Palm Beach.

Billie, James E. 1980. Interview by author, Hollywood Seminole Indian Reservation, February.

———. 1991. "Indian Days Festival" Presentation, Cory Osceola Family and Friends of the Collier County Museum, November 10, Naples.

———. 1995. Interview by author, Hollywood Seminole Indian Reservation, February 12.

Billie, Josie. 1932. Letter to J. F. Jaudon, September 5, J. F. Jaudon Papers, Historical Museum of Southern Florida, Miami, Fla.

Billie, Suzie Jim. 1990. Interview by author (Mary Jean Koenes, interpreter), Big Cypress Seminole Reservation, August 13.

Blackard, David M. 1990. *Patchwork and Palmettos: Seminole-Miccosukee Folk Art Since 1820*. Fort Lauderdale: Fort Lauderdale Historical Society.

Bowers, Elrod. 1998. "Tribe Sponsors Breakfast Details Tourist Attractions." *Seminole Tribune*, January 23. Seminole Tribe of Florida, Hollywood.

Bowers, Richard. 1993. Interview by author, Big Cypress Seminole Reservation, November 3.

Boyer, George F. 1974. Correspondence with author, July 12, Wildwood Historical Commission, Wildwood, N.J.

Bratley, Jessie H. 1911. Photo no. 489, Seminole/Miccosukee Photographic Archive, Fort Lauderdale.

Burghard, August. 1935. "Seminole Indians Ask Uncle Sam for New Deal." *Ft. Lauderdale News*, March 21.

Burman, Ben Lucien. 1956. "The Glamour of the Everglades." *Reader's Digest* 72:147–52.

———. 1959. "Florida's First Families—The Seminoles." *Reader's Digest* 75, no. 425 (December):196–204.

Burnstein, Jon. 2006. "Seminoles Snap up Hard Rock Empire." *Sun-Sentinel*, December 8.

———. 2007a. "Seminoles Have Grand Plans for Coconut Creek." *Sun-Sentinel*, January 23.

———. 2007b. "Seminoles Mark Largest Single Corporate Acquisition of any American Indian Tribe." *Sun-Sentinel*, March 6.

Buster, Andy. 1996a. Interview by author, Tamiami Trail, August 8.

———. 1996b. Telephone interview by author, September 16.

Buswell, James Oliver III. 1972. "Florida Seminole Religious Ritual: Resistance and Change." Ph.D. diss., St. Louis University. Ann Arbor, Mich.: University Microfilms.

Byrons Studio. 1916. Photos, Palm Beach Sundance of 1916. Private collection.

Campbell, Nellie M. 1981a. Telephone interview by author, January 10.

———. 1981b. Telephone interview by author, February 6.

Canadian National Exhibition. 1931. *Official Catalogue*. Canadian National Exhibition Archives, Toronto.

Capron, Louis. 1953. *The Medicine Bundles and Busks of the Florida Seminole and the Green Corn Dance*. Bureau of American Ethnology Anthropological Papers 35, no. 151:155–210. Washington: Government Printing Office.

Carter, Thomas. 1981. Interview by author, Coral Gables, June 12.

Cattelino, Jessica R. 2004. "High Stakes: Seminole Sovereignty in the Casino Era." Ph.D. diss., New York University, New York City.

Chicago Tribune. 1933. "Motorists Who Speed." March 10.

Cline, Howard F. 1974. *Provisional Historical Gazeteer with Localized Notes on Florida Colonial Communities, 1700–1823*. New York/London: Garland Publishing Company.

Comstock, Bertha. 1938. "Interview with J. D. Girtman." Typescript, Florida Collection, University of South Florida Library, Tampa.

Coppinger, Henry, Jr. 1931a. Press release. Private collection. Photocopy, Seminole/Miccosukee Photographic Archive, Fort Lauderdale.

———. 1931b. Receipt, private collection. Photocopy, Seminole/Miccosukee Photographic Archive, Fort Lauderdale.

———. 1931c. Telegram from Miami Chamber of Commerce to Henry Coppinger, Jr., August 11, 1932. Private collection. Photocopy, Seminole/Miccosukee Photographic Archive, Fort Lauderdale.

———. 1951. Letter to members, from Seminole Indian Association, November 20. Private collection. Photocopy, Seminole/Miccosukee Photographic Archive, Fort Lauderdale.

———. 1975. Interview by author, South Dade, June 13.

Cory, Charles Barney. 1896. *Hunting and Fishing in Florida*. Boston: Estes and Lauriat.

Courier-Journal. n.d. "Seminoles Now Tame Indians." Historical Museum of Southern Florida, clipping file, "Seminoles." Miami.

Craig, Alan K., and David McJunkin. 1971. "Stranahan's: Last of the Seminole Trading Posts." *The Florida Anthropologist* 24:45–50.

Creel, Lorenzo D. 1911. "Report of Special Agent of the Seminole Indians in Florida to the Commissioner of Indian Affairs." Washington.

Cypress, Billy. 1998. "Miccosukee Leader: Our houses won't harm ecology." *Miami Herald*, January 4.

Cypress, Billy L. 1996. Interview by author, Big Cypress Seminole Indian Reservation, September 5.

Cypress, Carol Frank. 1991. Interview by author, Chokoloskee, Fla., February 23.

Dade County Chancery Records. 1932. Book 88, Page 105, File 34405-D, Dade County Courthouse, Miami, Fla.

———. 1934. File 39284-C. November 13, Dade County Courthouse, Miami, Fla.

———. 1936. File 39234-C. January 21, Dade County Courthouse, Miami.

Davis, Alan W. 1980. Interview by author, Gulf Breeze, January 22.
———. 1981a. Telephone interview by author, February 19.
———. 1981b. Correspondence with author, March 10.
Davis, Eliose. 1996. "Economic Success Buys Cultural Preservation." *Business in Broward* (February):1–6.
Davis, Norma. 1926. "He Man Fever Spreads Fast at Indian Wedding Ceremony." *Miami News*, June 5.
Daytona Beach Independent. 1936. "Indians Get Chance to Earn Living." September 25.
Deloria, Vine, Jr., and Clifford Lytle. 1984. *The Nations Within: The Past and Future of American Indian Sovereignty.* New York: Pantheon Books.
Densmore, Frances. 1956. *Seminole Music.* Bureau of American Ethnology Bulletin 161. Washington: Government Printing Office.
deVane, Albert. 1978. *DeVane's Early Florida History.* Vols. 1 and 2. Sebring, Fla.: Sebring Historical Society.
Dimmock, Anthony Weston. 1908. *Florida Enchantments.* New York: The Outing Publishing Company.
Downs, Dorothy. 1981. "Coppinger's Tropical Gardens: The First Commercial Indian Village in Florida." *The Florida Anthropologist* 34:225–31.
Eagle Magazine. 1929. "Alligators and How!" August. Minneapolis.
Eliot, Samuel A. 1919. "Report on the Seminole Indians of Florida, By Samuel A. Eliot." *Report on the Board of Indian Commissioners*, Appendix L. March 15. Boston.
Fishbaugh, William A. 1922. Photo no. 482, February. Florida State Archives, Tallahassee.
Fletcher, Senator Duncan Udall. 1927. Letter of response to W. Stanley Hanson, February 12. Private collection. Photocopy, Seminole/Miccosukee Photographic Archive, Fort Lauderdale.
Florida Digest. 1935. "Florida Tribe Back to Springs." November 26. Orlando.
Florida Times Union (Jacksonville). 1937. "Seminoles Will Soon Resume Tribal Regalia." September 18.
Florida Writers' Project. 1941. *Seminole Indians in Florida.* Tallahassee: Florida State Department of Agriculture.
Ft. Myers News Press. 1930. "More Help for the Redskin." August 30.
———. 1935. "Seminoles Rescue Motorists after Dive into Trail Canal." March 2.
———. 1937a. "Trail Traffic Deaths Mount: State Aroused." March 14.
———. 1937b. "Seminoles Enact Sun Dance for Big Crowd at Bok Tower." March 15.
———. 1937c. "Hunting." March 27.
Ft. Pierce News Tribune. 1935. "Hunting." December 17.
Frank, Alexandra. 2001. "Seminole Hard Rock Café and Casino Forum." *Seminole Tribune*, September 7.
Franke, Kim. 1993. "Tore Up Thumbs. Mangled Toes. What drives a man to get in a scrap with a gator?" *Naples Daily News*, January 21.
Freeman, Ethel Cutler. 1938. Field notes. Ethel Cutler Freeman Papers, box 40. National Anthropological Archives, Smithsonian Institution.

————. 1939a. Diaries. Ethel Cutler Freeman Papers, ser. 5, box 43, January 11. National Anthropological Archives, Smithsonian Institution.

————. 1939b. Field notes. Ethel Cutler Freeman Papers, box 40. National Anthropological Archives, Smithsonian Institution.

————. 1939c. Map. Ethel Cutler Freeman Papers, box 40. National Anthropological Archives, Smithsonian Institution.

————. 1940. Ethel Cutler Freeman Papers, Series 5, Box 43, National Anthropological Archives, Smithsonian Institution.

————. 1941a. "Exhibition Camps." Ethel Cutler Freeman Papers, ser. 5, box 43. National Anthropological Archives, Smithsonian Institution.

————. 1941b. Diaries. Ethel Cutler Freeman Papers, ser. 5, box 43. National Anthropological Archives, Smithsonian Institution.

————. 1944. "The Seminole Woman of the Big Cypress and Her Influence in Modern Life." *America Indigena* 4, no. 2: 123–28. (Mexico; in English.)

————. 1947. "Our Unique Indians, the Seminoles of Florida." *American Indian* 21 (1944–45):14–28. Reprinted in *The American Eagle* 41, no. 49 (March 2):1–3, no. 50 (April 3):8–9. Estero, Fla.: Koreshan Unity.

Gallagher, Peter B. 1982. "Indian grapples with Alligator and white man's way." "Vanishing Florida," *St. Petersburg Times*, March 1.

————. 2007. "Jim Billie's Wild Ride." *Forum, The Magazine of the Florida Humanities Council* (Spring):26–29.

Gallagher, Tom. 1997. "Tourism Folks Have Wild Swamp Party." *Seminole Tribune*, February 21, Seminole Communications, Seminole Tribe of Florida, Hollywood.

Gehrke, Donna. 1997. "Miccosukees seek support for homes, Festival becomes forum for tribe." *Miami Herald*, July 22.

Glenn, James L. 1976. Typescript of interview by Marjorie D. Patterson with James Lafayette Glenn, Rockwall, Tex., October 22. Glenn Papers, Fort Lauderdale Historical Society.

————. 1982. *My Work among the Florida Seminoles.* Edited by Harry A. Kersey, Jr. Gainesville: University Presses of Florida.

Goodwin, Sue. 1946. Copy of letter to Director of Public Safety Dan Rosenfelder, forwarded to O. B. White, attorney, March 18. Historical Museum of Southern Florida, Miami Dade.

Greenlee, Robert F. 1952. "Aspects of Social Organization and Material Culture of the Seminoles of Big Cypress Swamp." *The Florida Anthropologist* 5, nos. 3–4:25–31.

Guttman, Martha Makemson. 1982. Interview by author. Ft. Lauderdale, May 24.

Hanna, Alfred Jackson, and Katheryn Abbey Hanna. 1948. *The American Lakes Series: Lake Okeechobee, Wellspring of the Everglades.* Indianapolis–New York: Bobbs-Merrill Company.

Hanson, Julia. 1909. Typescript of letter to Clara Amelia Petzold, Fort Myers, December 27. Private collection, W. Stanley Hanson Papers. Photocopy, Seminole/Miccosukee Photographic Archive, Fort Lauderdale.

Hanson, W. Stanley. 1927. Letter to Senator Duncan U. Fletcher, February 8. Private collection, W. Stanley Hanson Papers. Photocopy, Seminole/ Miccosukee Photographic Archive, Fort Lauderdale.

———. 1928. Letter to L. D. Reagin, editor, *Sarasota Times* (including transcript of a telegram), February 29. Private collection. Photocopy, Seminole/Miccosukee Photographic Archive, Fort Lauderdale.

———. 1934. Secretary's Report. Minutes, Seminole Indian Association. In *American Eagle*, Estero, Fla.: Koreshan Unity.

———. 1936. "Seminole Education." Filed in Indian Tribes/Reservations, Ethel Cutler Freeman Papers, box 43. National Anthropological Archives, Smithsonian Institution.

———. 1944. Letter to Ethel Cutler Freeman, March 1. Ethel Cutler Freeman Papers, Correspondence, box 40. National Anthropological Archives, Smithsonian Institution.

———. n.d. [ca. mid-1930s]. Typescript, undated letter to John Collier. Private collection, W. Stanley Hanson Papers. Photocopy, Seminole/ Miccosukee Photographic Archive, Fort Lauderdale.

Hanson, W. Stanley, and R. Carl Liddle. 1936. "Seminole (Commercial) Camps on Tamiami Trail Going from Fort Myers to Miami." September 28. Typescript, Ethel Cutler Freeman Papers, box 42B. National Anthropological Archives, Smithsonian Institution.

Hanton, Carl. 1936. "Governor Sholtz Makes Pact with the Seminoles at a Pow Wow in the Everglades He Comforts Indians Who Fear They'll Lose Villages." *Daytona Beach News Journal*, February 23.

Happenings in Miami. 1925. "Things You Should See." Vol. 2, no. 21 (April 5–11). Historical Museum of Southern Florida, Miami.

———. 1926. "Things You Should See." Vol. 4, no. 26 (May 16–22). In the collection of the Historical Museum of Southern Florida, Miami.

Hartford Courant. 1937. "Tamiami Trail in Florida Leads to Indian Villages." February 21.

Hartley, William, and Ellen Hartley. 1963. *A Woman Set Apart*. New York: Dodd, Meade.

Henry, Bobby. 1995. Interview by author, Hollywood Seminole Indian Reservation, February 11.

Hialeah Home News. 1964. Twentieth anniversary edition, April.

Higgens, Beth. 1982. Interview by author, Naples, November 22.

Holloway, Ruth. 1981. Interview by author, Coral Gables, November 17.

Hollywood Herald. 1936. "Indian Agent Lauds Seminole Tribesmen." October 23.

Homestead Enterprise. 1936. "Indian Hunters Warned Out of New Park Area." June 5.

Hutt, Katherine. 1997a. "Gold from Green, Tourism firms are working to meet travelers' demand to see Florida's natural side." *Sun Sentinel* (Fort Lauderdale), August 28.

———. 1997b. "Broward promoting ship-to-shore tourism." "Hospitality," *Sun Sentinel* (Fort Lauderdale), December 8.

International News Service. 1939. "Two Bullets to the Brain." May 27.

James, Phil. 1980. Interview by author, Avon Park, October 24.

———. 1981. Telephone interview, October 16.

Johns, Lena Cypress, and Betty Cypress. 1996. Interview by author (Mary F. Johns, interpreter), Brighton Seminole Indian Reservation, April 2.

Jones, Daryl. 1997. "Ecotourism: Nature's Way Is Best." *Seminole Tribune*, July 9, Hollywood.

Jumper, Alan. 1980. Interview by author, Hollywood Seminole Indian Reservation, February 16.

Jumper, Betty Mae. 1988. "Seminole Palmetto Dolls." *The Seminole Tribune*, January 11, Seminole Tribe of Florida, Hollywood.

———. 1994. *Legends of the Seminoles*. Sarasota: Pineapple Press.

Jumper, Betty Mae, and Patsy West. 2001. *Betty Mae Tiger Jumper: A Seminole Legend*. Gainesville: University Press of Florida.

Keesing, Roger M. 1989. "Creating the Past: Custom and Identity in the Contemporary Pacific." *The Contemporary Pacific* 1, nos. 1, 2 (Spring/Fall):19–42.

Kersey, Harry A., Jr. 1974. *A History of the Seminole and Miccosukee Tribes, 1959–1970*. U.S. Department of Commerce. Washington: National Technical Information Service PB 233 052.

———. 1975. *Pelts, Plumes and Hides: White Traders among the Seminole Indians, 1870–1930*. Gainesville: University of Florida Press.

———. 1981. "Florida Seminoles and the Census of 1900." *Florida Historical Quarterly* 60:145–60.

———. 1986. "Florida Seminoles in the Depression and New Deal, 1933–1942: An Indian Perspective." *Florida Historical Quarterly* 65:175–95.

———. 1989. *The Florida Seminoles and the New Deal, 1933–1942*. Boca Raton: Florida Atlantic University Press.

———. 1996. *An Assumption of Sovereignty, Social and Political Transformation among the Florida Seminoles, 1953–1979*. Lincoln/London:University of Nebraska Press.

King, R. Thomas. 1978. "The Florida Seminole Polity, 1858–1978." Ph.D. diss., University of Florida. Ann Arbor: University Microfilms.

Kleinberg, Howard. 1985. "Miami, The Way We Were: Musa Isle was early tourist lure." *Miami News*, April 13.

Lake Wales Daily. 1937. "[J. W.] Carson Reports Meeting at Fort Myers." March 4; "Seminole Indian Association Aims to Protect Game," March 12.

Lake Wales News. 1937. "Seminoles Are Naturalists." March 11.

Lantigua, John. 2007. "Gaming Lets Seminoles Turn Tables on Poverty." *Palm Beach Post*, February 4.

Lindsey, Sara. 1981. Telephone interview, June 29.

MacCauley, Clay. 1887. "The Seminole Indians of Florida." Fifth Annual Report of the Bureau of American Ethnology, 469–531. Washington: Government Printing Office.

Madison (Florida) *Recorder*. 1889. March 15.

Mail and Empire (Toronto). 1931. "Spectators at the C.N.E. Awed as Experts Fight Alligators." September 1.

Marriott, Alice L. 1943. "Arts and Crafts of the Florida Seminole." *Reports and Documents Concerning the Indian Arts and Crafts Board* 7 (December 1):47–58. Washington: Department of the Interior.

Martin, Wilton. 1937. "Silver Springs Bubbles." *Ocala Star*, March 3.

Matlack, Claude C. 1921. Photographic register, Claude C. Matlack Collection. Historical Museum of Southern Florida, Miami.

McClare, Kate. 1979. "Attention, Please." "That's Really Incredible!" *Ft. Lauderdale News*, n.d.

McGoun, Bill A. 1972. *A Biographic History of Broward County*. Miami: Miami Herald.

McIver, Stuart A. 1988. *Glimpses of South Florida History*. Miami: Florida Flare Books.

———. 1993. "The Long Sleep of Jack Tiger Tail." *Sunshine: The Magazine of South Florida*, August 1. Ft. Lauderdale: Sun Sentinel.

Meriam Report. 1928. *The Problem of Indian Administration*. Edited by Lewis Meriam. Brookings Institution, Institute for Government Research. Baltimore: John Hopkins University Press.

Miami Beach Tribune. 1935. "Recovery of Victim Assured." April 30.

Miami Chamber of Commerce. 1927. "Forward to the Soil." Program, February 5, no. 87.5.1, Seminole/Miccosukee Photographic Archive, Fort Lauderdale.

Miami Daily News. 1925. "Papoose Christened Ta-Ha-Ma By Indian, White Man's Rites." July 12.

———. 1927. "At Muck Land Ceremonies." February 6.

———. 1930a. "Bootleg Liquor and White Men Said Debauching Dade Indians, Commissioner Depicts Condition of Seminoles Especially Women in 'Villages' Back of Miami." August 25.

———. 1930b. "Seminole Leaders Disagree Upon Charges Made by Ucker, Tony Tommie Accuses White Moonshiners and Cory Osceola Discounts Story Told by Federal Indian Commissioner." August 29.

———. 1930c. "Hoover's Move is Challenged by Seminoles, Chief Cory Osceola Wires President Against Land Transfers." N.d.

———. 1931. "Miami Display Loaded for Canada Fair." July 29.

———. 1935. "Red Men Start Rebuilding Huts Lost in Flames." October 28.

———. 1938a. "Indian Ruler Claims Victim Beat Daughter." February 24.

———. 1938b. "Osceola Awaits Verdict of Tribesmen in Slaying." February 25.

———. 1938c. "Seminole & Paleface Laws Clash—Execution of Johnny Billie Decreed by Tribal Court, Members Will Testify in Defense of Patriarch." March 2.

———. 1938d. "Jury Says 'Justifiable Homicide' After Brief Deliberation." March 4.

———. 1938e. "Seminoles Feast to Celebrate Acquittal of Chief Osceola." March 6.

———. 1940. "Indian Commissioner Collier Hears Seminole Plea for Deer." January 5.

———. 1962. "John A. Roop." July 16.

Miami Herald. 1911a. "Little Indian Baby Died at Hospital." February 15.

———. 1911b. "Successful Season." April 1.

———. 1917a. "Miami Hit by Freeze." February 4–5.

———. 1917b. "Fifteen Days King's Party Now Past Due." March 11.

———. 1922a. "Picturesque Tropical Gardens Invite Visitors to Gaze on Native Florida." January 22.

———. 1922b. "Seminole Wedding." January 29.

———. 1922c. "Seminole Keep Fires Burning." March 9.

———. 1922d. "Lone Seminole Sees Slain Chief Buried by Palefaces and Grunts Tribe's Approval." March 10.

———. 1922e. "The New Head of the Tigertail Seminole Village." March 15.

———. 1922f. "Seminole Planning to Stay in Village on Edge of 'Glades." March 15.

———. 1922g. "Tiger Tail Fund." March 31.

———. 1926a. "Chief Will Take Wife." May 31.

———. 1926b. "Seminole Chief Weds: 2,000 Persons See Seminole Wedding at Musa Isle Village." June 4.

———. 1926c. "Seminole Chief Asks Citizenship for Tribe." November 27.

———. 1927. "Newsreel." January 31.

———. 1928a. "Indian Buried in White Cemetery." February 18.

———. 1928b. "Tony Tommie Grieves Alone in Everglades—Seminole Leader Disappears After Death of Wife." February 19.

———. 1930. "Commission to View Seminole Villages—Musa Isle Operator and Indian Protest Statement Alleging Spread of Disease." November 11.

———. 1931. "Miami in Canada." September 8.

———. 1933. "Statistics." December 20.

———. 1934. "Mickey Welcomes Seminole Children." September 8.

———. 1935. "End of 100 Year War of Seminoles Nearing." March 20.

———. 1937. "Indian Show Camps in Miami Protested, Seminoles Exhibited 'Like Monkeys or Alligators,' Says Missionary." March 6.

———. 1938a. "Police See Law Appeased by Verdict in Osceola Case." March 6.

———. 1938b. "Seminole Indian Camp at Wild Bill's Zoo Will Attract Visitors." January 2.

———. 1939. "All Aboard for the World's Fair." April 17.

———. 1940. "Governor Joins Cattlemen in Tick-Infested Deer Fight." March 9.

———. 1982. "Seminoles ready to wrestle state over 'gator farm." June 6.

———. 1983. "Indians' profits go politicking: The Seminoles cashing in on sovereignty." May 30.

Miami Metropolis. 1915a. "Seminole Indians in Peculiar Celebration of Christmas Season—Aborigines Will Tonight Begin Their Wild Dances to Continue for Week—Camp at Fifth and River." December 24.

———. 1915b. "Formal Opening Sunday of the Alligator Farm." December 18.

Miami Post. 1930. "Leave the Seminoles Alone." November 29.

Miccosukee Tribe of Indians of Florida. 1997. "Should The National Park Service

Be Allowed to Destroy Generations of Indian Culture?" *Naples Daily News*, December 6.

Minch, Jack. 1997. "Maiden Flight." *Ft. Pierce Tribune*, December 18.

Mitchell, Virginia Bert. 1998. Interview by author. Hollywood Seminole Indian Reservation, February 20.

Musa Isle. ca. 1929. Brochure. No. 92.24.1, Seminole/Miccosukee Photographic Archive, Fort Lauderdale.

Nash, Roy. 1931. *Survey of the Seminole Indians of Florida*. Senate Document 314, 71st Cong., 1st sess. Washington: Government Printing Office.

Newsweek. 1942. "Stalked Deer." 19, no. 33 (March 16).

New York Times. 1924. "Florida's Exhibition Draws Large Crowd, Seminole Indians from Collier County See Their First Snow, Fruit Given Away." February 19.

———. 1935. "After 100 Years Seminoles Offer Peace." March 17.

———. 1939. "Two Bullets in the Brain, New York Wrestling Bout Fatal to Gator." May 27.

Nunez, Theron. 1989. "Touristic Studies in Anthropological Perspective." In *Hosts and Guests: The Anthropology of Tourism*, 2d ed., ed. Valene L. Smith, 265–74. Philadelphia: University of Pennsylvania Press.

Ober, Frederick A. 1875. "Ten Days with the Seminoles." *Appleton's Journal of Literature, Science and Art* 14 (July–December):328–53.

Ocala Morning Banner. 1930. "Devoted to Indian Service." August 19.

Okeechobee News. 1939. "Thirty-seven Seminoles Dine in Circle on Floor of New York Station." April 21.

———. 1996. "Florida Seminole tourism introduced at trade show." February 26.

Oliver, James. 1931. "The Burial of Tony Tommie." Typescript with handwritten notes, Fort Lauderdale Historical Society.

Orlando Sentinel. 1987. "Seminoles Open Doors with Hotel." February 5.

———. 1998. "Alligator wrestler puts a little bite into his show." January 2.

Osceola, Cory R. 1975. Interview by author, Miami, November 20.

Osceola, Dan. 1995. Interview by author, Hollywood Seminole Indian Reservation, February 11.

Osceola, Howard. 1995. Interview by David M. Blackard, Hollywood Seminole Indian Reservation, February 11.

Osceola, Jimmie O. 1991. Telephone interview, April 29.

———. 1996a. Interview by author, Hollywood Seminole Indian Reservation, January 24.

———. 1996b. Interview by author, Hollywood Seminole Indian Reservation, August 29.

———. 1996c. Telephone interview, September 18.

Osceola, Juanita Cypress. 1985. Interview by author, (O. B. White Osceola, interpreter), Golden Gate, Fla., November 10.

Osceola, Larry Mike. 1982. Interview by author, Le Canto, Fla., January 31.

Osceola, Laura Mae. 1991. Interview by author, Hollywood Seminole Indian Reservation, February 9.

Osceola, O. B. White, Sr. 1985. Interview by author, Golden Gate, Fla., October 10.

———. 1987. Interview by author, Naples, Fla., November 21.

Osceola, Pete, Sr. 1983. Interview by author, Naples, November 19.

Palm Beach Post. 1930. "Indians Disagree on Ucker Claim." August 30.

———. 1936. "Annual Sun Dance to be Given Here This Week." March 15.

Parrott, J. R. 1900. Letter to J. E. Ingraham, November 21, box 21-A, Flagler Archives, Palm Beach.

Philip, Kenneth R. 1977. "Turmoil at Big Cypress: Seminole Deer and the Florida Cattle Tick Controversy." *Florida Historical Quarterly* 56 (July):28–44.

Redman, Virginia Roop Bloodsworth. 1981. Interview by author, Miami Shores, February 21.

Resorts. 1938. "Seminoles by the Road, along the Tamiami Trail They Lie in Wait to Welcome the Tourists." January 9, [n.p.].

Romer, Gleason Waite. 1927. Photographs in series, nos. 153 k-l, Romer Photographic Collection, Florida Room, Miami-Dade Library System, Miami, Fla.

St. Pete Independent. 1935. "Indian Court of Medicine Men Offers to Try Seminole Buck Accused of Killing Tribesman." July 27.

St. Petersburg Daily News. 1927. "Seminole Chief Denounces Tony Tommie as 'Fakir and Traitor'." February 14.

———. 1937. "Seminoles Draw Much Attention at Pier Camp." March 5.

St. Petersburg Times. 1937a. "Seminole Indians Plan Local Visit." March 2.

———. 1937b. "Indians Here Appear at Pier." March 4.

Sainz, Adrian. "Seminole Tribe Completes Hard Rock Deal." *Palm Beach Post*, March 13.

Schulberg, Budd. 1958. *Wind Across the Everglades*. Movie. Warner Bros., no. 58–343.

Seminole Agency, Florida. 1977. *Florida Seminoles Reconstructed Census Roll of 1914.* May 20. Pp. 1–138. William D. and Edith M. Boehmer Papers, Seminole/Miccosukee Photographic Archive, Fort Lauderdale.

"Seminole Indians." ca. 1935. Unidentified newspaper clipping, Historical Museum of Southern Florida, Miami.

Seminole/Miccosukee Photographic Archive Collection. ca. 1900. Photo no. 710, Billy Bowlegs and Friend. Seminole/Miccosukee Photographic Archives, Fort Lauderdale.

———. ca. 1911. Photos in series, nos. 462–463, Little Billie and family at Fort Myers fair. Seminole/Miccosukee Photographic Archives, Fort Lauderdale.

———. 1932a. Photo no. 975, Entrance to Seminole Village, Wildwood, N.J. Seminole/Miccosukee Photographic Archives, Fort Lauderdale.

———. 1932b. Photo no. 739, Entrance to Canadian National Exhibition. Seminole/Miccosukee Photographic Archives, Fort Lauderdale.

Sessa, Frank Bowman. 1951. "Miami on the Eve of the Boom: 1923." *Tequesta* 11:3–25. Historical Association of Southern Florida, Miami, Fla.

Skinner, Alanson. 1913. "Notes on the Florida Seminole." *American Anthropologist* 15:63–77.

Smiley, Nixon. 1967. "Irishman First Gator Wrestler." *Miami Herald*, February 26.

———. 1968. "Yes, Miami River Once Had 'Falls'." *Miami Herald*, June 30.

Smith, Mac. 1959. "Deaconess, 83, Brings Christ to the Seminoles." *Miami News*, January 11.

Smith, Valene L. 1989. Editor's preface, *Hosts and Guests: The Anthropology of Tourism*, 2d ed. Editor's preface, ix–xi, Introduction, 1–17. Philadelphia: University of Pennsylvania Press.

Snel, Alan. 1998. "Miccosukees Put Big Bucks into Sports Marketing." *Sun-Sentinel*, July 22.

Spencer, Lucien A. 1913. "Seminole Indians in Florida, Letter of the Acting Commissioner of Indian Affairs to Senator Duncan U. Fletcher." Senate Document 42, 63d Cong., 1st sess. Washington: Government Printing Office.

Spoehr, Alexander. 1941. *Camp, Clan, and Kin among the Cow Creek Seminoles of Florida*. Anthropological Series, Field Museum of Natural History, 33:121–50.

Staats, Eric. 1997a. "Miccosukee ads highlight park struggle." *Naples Daily News*, December 4.

———. 1997b. "Miccosukee Indians buy 800 acres in Collier County. The Indians say they will preserve the land for use in tribal customs." *Naples Daily News*, December 25.

Starts, Captain Al. 1986. Interview by author, Fort Lauderdale, July 9.

Stewart, Billy. 1923. Telegram to Henry Coppinger, Jr., Miami, Fla., May. Private collection, Coppinger Papers. Photocopy, Seminole/Miccosukee Photographic Archive, Fort Lauderdale.

Stipulation. 1939. Document no. 93.45.1, April 13, O. B. White Papers, Seminole/Miccosukee Photographic Archive, Fort Lauderdale.

Stirling, Gene. 1936. *Report on the Seminole of Florida*. Office of Indian Affairs, Applied Anthropology Unit, Washington.

Storm, Mary Jane Cypress. 1985. Interview by author, Big Cypress, September 8.

Stout, Wesley. n.d. Wesley Stout Papers, Fort Lauderdale Historical Society, Fort Lauderdale.

Stranahan, Frank. 1900. Letter to J. E. Ingraham, November 19. Ivy C. Stranahan Papers, Fort Lauderdale Historical Society.

Sturtevant, William C. 1955. "The Mikasuki Seminole: Medical Beliefs and Practices." Ph.D. diss., Yale University. Ann Arbor: University Microfilms, 1967.

———. 1956. "A Seminole Personal Document." *Tequesta* 16:55–75. Historical Association of Southern Florida, Miami.

———. 1967. "The Mikasuki Seminole: Medical Beliefs and Practices." Ph.D. diss., Yale University. University Microfilms, Ann Arbor.

———. 1971. "Creek into Seminole." In *North American Indians in Historical Perspective*, edited by Eleanore Burke Leacock and Nancy Oestreich Lurie, 92–128. New York: Random House.

————. 1997. Correspondence with the author, October 21.

Suarez, Yeleny. 2007. "Ready to Rock." *South Florida CEO* (March):37–42.

Tallahassee Democrat. 1935. "Huge Indian Dies in Crash," August 18.

Tampa Tribune. 1935. "Silver Springs Wins Claim as Number 1 Lure." December 1.

————. 1936. "Seminoles Move to Mountain Lake." March 15.

Tebeau, Charlton W. 1957. *Florida's Last Frontier: The History of Collier County*. Miami: University of Miami Press.

Tiger, Lee. 1997. "Seminole Tourism Spotlighted at Brit World Travel Market." *Seminole Tribune*, December 19, Seminole Tribe of Florida, Hollywood.

————. 1998. "'Seminole Swamp Party' in Iceland." *Seminole Tribune*, March 6.

Tiger, Mary. 1982. Interview by author, Naples, November 15.

Tolstoy, J. 1941. Memorandum from J. Tolstoy, Marine Studios, Marineland, Fla., to Vernon Lamme, November 26. Records Relating to Technical Assistance, 1932–48, box 2, RG 435, "Nationwide Survey for Potential Directory of Currently Produced Indian Goods." Washington: National Archives.

Toronto Star Weekly. 1931. "Pretty Bride from Jungle Adept in Can-opener Menu." September 1.

Tropical Sun. 1895. "Here and There." Juno, Fla. February 14.

Ucker, Clement S. 1930. *Report on the Seminole Indians of Florida*, submitted to Hon. Samuel A. Eliot, Board of Indian Commissioners, July 9, 1–5.

U.S. Congress. 1897. Executive Document. *Report of Indians in Florida*, 125–27.

————, House. 1897. *Report of the Commissioner of Indian Affairs*. Exec. Doc. 5, 55th Cong., 2d sess. Washington: Government Printing Office.

————. 1898. *Report of the Commissioner of Indian Affairs*. Exec. Doc. 5, 33d Cong., 3d sess. Exhibit G. Report of A. J. Duncan, U.S. Indian Inspector, to the Honorable Secretary of the Interior, in Regard to the Reservation of Lands for Use of the Seminole Indians in Florida, cc–ccxxxviii.

————. 1954. *Termination of Federal Supervision Over Certain Tribes of Indians, Joint Hearing Before the Subcommittee of the Committees on Interior and Insular Affairs, 83rd Cong., 2nd Sess*. On S. 2747 and H.R. 7321, Part 8, Seminole Indians of Florida, March 1–2. Washington: Government Printing Office.

U.S. Department of the Interior, Office of Indian Affairs. 1896. *Annual Report*. Commissioner of Indian Affairs, 54th Cong., 2d sess., House Documents 3489:55.

————. 1913. *Annual Report*. Seminole Agency, Dania, Fla.

————. 1915. *Annual Report*. Seminole Agency, Dania, Fla.

————. 1917. *Interior Department Report*. "Exhibition," 65th Cong., 2d sess., House Documents 7358:41.

————. 1918. *Annual Report*. Seminole Agency, Dania, Fla.

————. 1919. *Annual Report*. Seminole Agency, Dania, Fla.

————. 1925. *Annual Report*. Seminole Agency, Dania, Fla.

————. 1927. *Annual Report*. Seminole Agency, Dania, Fla.

————. 1932. *Annual Report*. Seminole Agency, Dania, Fla.

————. 1933. *Annual Report*. Seminole Agency, Dania, Fla.

———. 1935. *Annual Report.* Seminole Agency, Dania, Fla.

Valentine, Twila. 1997. "C-Okee Group planning extensive major projects." *Okeechobee News*, October 30.

Varma, Kavita. 1997. "Like Spring break, tourist season is a thing of the past, says Ft. Lauderdale tourism chief." *Broward Business Journal*, November 28.

Wardlow, Jean. 1969. "Indians, Animals Long Gone, Tropical Paradise Is Closing." *Miami Herald*, January 29.

Warren, Cecil R. 1934. *Florida's Seminoles.* Reprinted from Warren's *Miami Daily News* Special Investigative Series. Miami: Stirling Press.

Washburn, Wilcomb E. 1975. *The Indian in America.* New York: Harper and Row.

West, Patsy. 1981. "The Miami Indian Tourist Attractions: A History and Analysis of a Transitional Mikasuki Seminole Environment." *The Florida Anthropologist* 34, no. 4 (December):200–224.

———. 1982. "Seminole Totem Poles?" *New River News* 21, no. 2 (Fall):16. Fort Lauderdale Historical Society.

———. 1983. "The Woman in Seminole Society." Paper presented at the Florida Anthropological Society Annual Meeting, Tallahassee.

———. 1984. "Glade Cross Mission: An Influence on Seminole Arts and Crafts." *American Indian Art Magazine* 9, no. 4 (Autumn):58–67. Scottsdale, Arizona.

———. 1985. "Seminoles in Broward County: The Pine Island Legacy." *New River News* 23 (Fall):4–11. Ft. Lauderdale Historical Society.

———. 1986a. "Blind Pass Seminole Village." *Seminole Tribune*, "Reflections," no. 17, February 10. Seminole Communications, Seminole Tribe of Florida, Hollywood.

———. 1986b. "Introduced Crafts and Totem Poles." *Seminole Tribune*, "Reflections," no. 20, March 10. Seminole Communications, Seminole Tribe of Florida, Hollywood.

———. 1986c. "The Seminole Arts and Crafts Center." *Seminole Tribune*, "Reflections," no. 28, July. Seminole Communications, Seminole Tribe of Florida, Hollywood.

———. 1987a. "Doing the Boats." *Seminole Tribune*, "Reflections," no. 43, April 6. Seminole Communications, Seminole Tribe of Florida, Hollywood.

———. 1987b. "Cory Osceola: Historical Sketch." Presentation, "Indian Days Festival," Cory Osceola Family and Friends of the Collier County Museum, November, Naples, Fla.

———. 1989. "Seminole Indian Settlements at Pine Island, Broward County, Florida: An Overview." *The Florida Anthropologist* 32, no.1:43–56.

———. 1992a. "Miami's muck land promotion threatened Seminole sovereignty." *South Florida History Magazine* 19, no. 1 (Winter):16–26.

———. 1992b. "The Seminole Old Tiger Tail and the Period of Isolation." *The Florida Anthropologist* 45, no. 4 (December):363–68.

———. 1993. "Seminole Warriors in the 20th Century." Paper read at the Annual Meeting of the Florida Historical Society, May 21, Pensacola.

———. 1994. "W. Stanley Hanson: White Medicine Man." Paper read at the Annual Meeting of the Florida Historical Society, May 21, Fort Myers.

———. 1995a. "At Home on the Res." *Seminole Tribune*, "Reflections," no. 90, March 10. Seminole Tribe of Florida, Hollywood.

———. 1995b. "Betty Mae Jumper." Paper read at the Annual Meeting of the Florida Historical Society, May 19, Tallahassee.

———. 1996. "*i.laponki.:* The Florida Seminoles in the 1930's." *Native Peoples Magazine* 9, no. 3 (Spring):26–33. Phoenix.

———. 1997. "Museum Notes." *Seminole Tribune*, October 3. Seminole Communications, Seminole Tribe of Florida, Hollywood.

———. 1998 (in press). "Reviving Florida's 'Native' Crafts." In *Peacocks and Palmetto Fans: Southern Craft and American Identity*, edited by Eileen Borris and Jane Becker. Columbia: McKissick Museum, University of South Carolina.

———. 2001. Personal Notes, "Seminole Fair," February.

———. 2007a. "From Hard Times to Hard Rock." *Forum, The Magazine of the Florida Humanities Council* (Spring):10–16.

———. 2007b. Personal Notes. "Hollywood, Florida," March 4.

———. 2007c. "Tiger Tiger Rocks." *Forum, The Magazine of the Florida Humanities Council* (Spring):34–35.

White, O. B.. 1946. Letter in response to Sue Goodwin, March 20, Historical Museum of Southern Florida, Miami.

Wildwood Leader. 1932. "The Indians Are Coming! Seminole Indians and Alligators Direct from Florida." May 26, Wildwood, N.J.

Wiley, Nancy. 1985. *The Great State Fair of Texas: An Illustrated History*. Dallas: Taylor Publishing Company.

Willoughby, Capt. Hugh O. 1898. *Across the Everglades: A Canoe Journey of Exploration*. Philadelphia: Lippincott.

Willson, Minnie Moore. 1910. *The Seminoles of Florida*. Philadelphia: America Printing House.

Wing, Bishop Right Rev. John D. 1933. Letter to Deaconess Harriet M. Bedell, April 28, Historical Museum of Southern Florida, Miami.

Winter, Nevin O. 1918. *Florida: The Land of Enchantment*. Boston.

Works Progress Administration (WPA). 1930. Material in WPA files of the Florida Historical Society, Cocoa.

Yari, Ethel. 1999. "James Billie Seminole Chief Leads his Tribe into the 21 Century." *Florida Living* (July).

Young, Tandy. 1996. "Guest Essay." *Native Peoples Magazine* (January–March):5. Phoenix.

Collier County: deer ticks remain in, 90; *i:laponathli:* camps in, 21, 84; *i:laponathli:* councilmen residing in, 79; Miccosukee Tribe's purchase of property in, 117; movement of Big Cypress Indians into, 84; nonreservation *i:laponathli:* living in, 113; residents in Miami attractions, 61; "Trail Blazers" in, 83
Columbus Sesquicentennial, 117
Committee on Indian Affairs, 80
commoditization, 31, 70, 73, 94–95
Conant, Henry, 64
Cone, Fred P., 91
Conners, W. J., 61
Conrad, Charlotte, 37
coonti, 4, 15, 51
Copeland, D. Graham, 84
Coppinger, Henry, Jr.: as "Alligator Boy" alligator wrestler, 13, 16, 42, 44; Alligator Farm, 16; as alligator wrestler, Canada (1931–32), 64, 65; at Coppinger's Alligator Farm, 16; and expo trip taking Seminoles to Canada (1931), 62–64; as member of Seminole Indian Association, 106; as mourner at Tiger Tail funeral, 36; on origins of Seminole camp at Coppinger's 14; rivalry with Musa Isle over alligators, 16; rivalry with Willie Willie, 16
Coppinger, Henry, Sr., 12
Coppinger, Mrs. Henry, Sr., 24
Coppinger, Jack, 64
Coppinger, Sonny, 56
Coppinger's Alligator Farm, 16, 18, 42, 43, 44–45
Coppinger's Pirates Cove Indian Village (1922)/(Coppinger's Tiger Tail Indian Village, 1922–26): and the carving of totem poles (1928), 56; discussed (1932), 24; faces government opposition in report (1930), 96–97; and government assessment (1936), 100–101; headmen at, 76; murder at (1922), 35–36, 38; as newspaper feature (1922), 18; in 1926 hurricane, 23; in 1950s, 111; promoted by City of Miami, 21; in retrospect, 112; and salary (1930), 28–29. *See also* Coppinger's Tropical Gardens
Coppinger's Trading Post (craft shop), 44, 53

Coppinger's Tropical Gardens (1917), 12, 13, 14, 105; headmen at, 76. *See also* Coppinger's Pirates Cove Indian Village
Cow Creek camps, 2, 78
crafts. *See* arts and crafts
Creek speakers. *See ci:saponathli:*
Creel, Lorenzo D., 8
crop picking. *See* economy
cross-cultural conflicts/misconceptions: regarding ambition, 27; regarding land, 6; regarding work, 107
Crow, Lon Worth, 72, 73
Cuba: and Miccosukees, 113; and Seminole economics, 121
cultural tourism. *See* tourism
cultural traits: regarding abnormal behavior, 27, 40; regarding ambition, 27; regarding confrontations, 7
culture broker, 109–10
Curtis, Glenn, 20
customs. *See* folkways
Cypress, Billy L. (Bear), 125
Cypress, Charlie (Otter), 23–24, 26
Cypress, Elvis "Tippy" (*Tahkoshathee*), 47
Cypress, Futch (Otter), 21
Cypress, Mrs. Futch (Panther), 28
Cypress, Henry (Panther), 63
Cypress, John (Panther), 26, 90
Cypress, Kenny (Bird), 47, 116
Cypress, Lee (Panther), 24
Cypress, Ruby (Panther), 21
Cypress, Tihokee Osceola (Otter), 63
Cypress, Whitney (Otter), 26
Cypress, Wilson (Otter), 26

Dade Battle commemoration, 81, 89
Dade County, 79, 83
Dade Massacre, 79
Dania, 6
Dania/Hollywood Reservation: and alligator wrestlers, 46, 48; and Big City Island, 7; and burial of nonreservation Indians, 37; craft shops on, 111; as haven, 38; housing at, 48; intoxication and violence at, 101; population of, 76–77, 78, 103; school at, 77; and totem poles, 56; women sell crafts at Miami attractions, 52
—residents of, 89; at Indian village on New

The Florida History and Culture Series
Edited by Raymond Arsenault and Gary R. Mormino